HEALTHY
BOARDS

◆

SUCCESSFUL
SCHOOLS

Praise for *Healthy Boards, Successful Schools*

"Bill Mott understands the critical role that trustees play in independent schools: Healthy and sustainable schools have healthy and sustainable board cultures. He recognizes that board actions today set the path and the tone for the school's future. His experience in working with boards is extensive; and his advice is practical, clear, and very wise."

R. Kirk Walker Jr., Ph.D.
Past President, Southeastern Association of
Independent Schools (SAIS), Atlanta, GA

"Because all leadership is reflective, the health of the board is on full display throughout every aspect of the school. Solomon said, 'If people can't see what God is doing, they stumble all over themselves; But when they attend to what he reveals, they are most blessed' (Proverbs 19:18 The Message). *Healthy Boards, Successful Schools* is a very practical guide for board members and school leaders to gain a better understanding of God's plan for the school and how to implement it. Dr. Mott's use of case stories is simply masterful! Working through these together will allow the board to become proactive instead of reactive, ready to overcome difficult challenges and embrace strategic opportunities to fulfill God's purpose for the school."

Stephen G. Reel, Ph.D.
Head of School, Mitchell Road Academy,
Greeneville, SC

"In my twenty-one years of headship, the importance of healthy, well-functioning, and strategic boards has never been more vital to the overall health of independent schools. Bill Mott has become one of the most respected voices in our profession about this critical facet of school life. Bill's new book, *Healthy Boards, Successful Schools*, represents the next chapter in his course on how to build and maintain this essential quality of successful schools. Bravo and thank you, Bill, for another must-read."

Scott Wilson
Former Headmaster, Baylor School,
Chattanooga, TN

"To say Bill Mott understands governance is an absurd under-statement. He has been a board member, a board chair, and a head of school. He has traveled the country working with school heads and boards for years. His goal is to help independent and faith-based schools be their best. What most impresses me is Bill's incredible ability to combine a 'down-home charm' with a hard-headed approach to governance. *Healthy Boards, Successful Schools* is accessible whilst also laying out concrete directives on how best to govern schools. In an age where governance issues seem to pop up more and more, this book needs to be required reading for school leaders and board members nationwide. He manages to reframe what can often be tension-filled situations into opportunities for school leadership to partner on provid-ing strategic leadership and setting a school's course into the future."

David Colon
Head of School, Visitation Academy, St. Louis, MO

"This book addresses many vital issues that independent schools face in today's private school culture. Dr. Mott's vast knowledge gained from working with various independent schools over the course of many years is very insightful regarding the struggles many schools experience. The case studies are well thought out and presented in an interesting and applicable way that is relevant to all independent schools. As the chair of the board of trustees of Providence Christian Academy, I have had the unique opportunity to work with Dr. Mott and see the measurable results of applying his principles. Our school has grown under his leadership to one of the fastest-growing independent schools in the country, and I firmly believe that this growth would not have occurred if we were not practicing the principles laid out in this book. An independent school, whether faith-based or college preparatory, cannot thrive in a healthy atmosphere unless the head and the board of trustees work together in a healthy manner. *Healthy Boards, Successful Schools* is a must-read for all leaders involved in independent schools."

Julie Knox
Past Chair of the Board of Trustees,
Providence Christian Academy, Murfreesboro, TN

"Bill Mott tackles the subject of board governance and leadership with creative flair. In *Healthy Boards, Successful Schools* Dr. Mott infuses the essentials of good governance into very digestible case study examples, while taking a deeper and broader dive into this vital topic for schools than most books do."

Jeff Mitchell, Ph.D.
Head of School, Currey Ingram Academy,
Brentwood, TN

"Bill Mott's compelling and timely investigation of the most critical challenges facing independent school governing boards today is filled with insights to support the work of school leaders and trustees. *Healthy Boards, Successful Schools* succinctly and clearly distills the principles to follow that will ensure long-term stability and strength in leading schools and carrying out a school's distinct mission and purpose. In today's world with the dynamics of constant change, a strong school must have a strong foundation of leadership—starting with the head of school and each member of the board of trustees. Dr. Mott's advice will guide each person in serving as a leader to carry out his or her responsibilities with clarity and unity of purpose. This book is essential for school trustees and heads of school who desire to learn and grow and make a lasting impact on their schools through extraordinary governance."

Larry McLemore, Ph.D.
Head of School, Saint James School, Montgomery, AL

"Bill Mott has authored a must-read for current or potential trustees of independent schools. More than any other single factor in independent schools, thoughtful, prepared, and visionary trustees are necessary to ensure that governance supports the mission of these incredibly important institutions. Dr. Mott continues to expertly and comprehensively provide independent school trustees with the necessary skills and warnings to work with leadership to ensure that their schools' missions are available to the next generation."

Jim McIntyre
President, Lake Highland Preparatory School,
Orlando, FL

"Here it is—the trifecta of board governance literature. Dr. Bill Mott has done it again. His third book, *Healthy Boards, Successful Schools*, is practical, meaningful, and fresh board leadership training pulled straight from the real world. Transformative principals are what you will encounter in the pages to follow. If you are wondering how to manage issues of board members knowing how to be great board members and heads of school operating in a clear, mission-driven environment—this book is a must-read! The case stories will allow you to learn invaluable lessons without having to endure many of the missteps described here. Don't miss out. Read this book. Have a better board, a better school."

Hugh Harris
Headmaster, Franklin Christian Academy,
Franklin, TN

"Bill Mott's new book is an impressive and comprehensive examination of what makes independent and faith-based private schools thrive. The answer—to create and maintain a healthy board culture—is not new. But what is new is the author's deep understanding and lucid explanations of board structure and operations, coupled with multiple compelling case stories drawn from his own work with boards, and astute analysis of what happens when best practices are followed—and when they are not. Without a doubt, *Healthy Boards, Successful Schools* is the most useful and user-friendly book on independent school governance I have seen—a must-have, must-read for all independent and private school leaders."

Richard Martin, Ph.D.
Former Executive Director, Tennessee Association
of Independent Schools (TAIS), Brentwood, TN

"Dr. William Mott has a long and impressive background in independent school education, and he truly understands governance and its importance to the proper and effective management of schools. Dr. Mott provides deep insights and practical advice for school leaders and independent school boards of all sizes, whether the school is classical, traditional, or progressive in curricular and pedagogical makeup. Nothing is more important to the life of a school than its governance structure and practice. This book is a terrific guide to help new and established schools better understand and implement good governance. From understanding the role and makeup of the board to establishing generative boards, *Healthy Boards, Successful Schools* is a must-read for independent school leaders and boards alike."

Timothy P. Wiens, Ed.D.
Headmaster, Mount Paran Christian School,
Kennesaw, GA

"As the saying goes, everything rises and falls on leadership. In his third book on board governance, Dr. Bill Mott gives us his best, most comprehensive work yet! *Healthy Boards, Successful Schools* leverages Bill's years of experience as a school leader and consultant, tackling the critically important role of the board of trustees. Replete with case studies and practical examples of what works and what doesn't, this is a must-read for school leaders and board members who truly want to grow in their understanding of what it means to lead and govern effectively."

C. David Balik, Ed.D.
Vice President, USA, Association of Christian
Schools International (ACSI), Colorado Springs, CO

"Today, a head of school's position is akin to a super hero, and most cannot relate to their work, except perhaps the board chair and the trustees. Bill Mott demystifies this relationship and validates the importance of strong governance by sharing ample case stories and text to give insights that are sure to help any current or prospective school leader (trustee or administrator)."

John Thorsen
Head of School, Athens Academy, Athens, GA

"As director of a state association of independent schools, I am keenly aware of the significance of leadership and governance issues for the survival—all the more, the success—of independent schools. That's why I often turn to Bill Mott and why I refer schools to him. Bill is the go-to guy on issues regarding leadership and governance in independent schools. Whether as a private consultant or through his books and seminars, Bill dispenses sensible advice that schools would be wise to heed when they seek to attain levels of success previously unattainable."

A. Shane Blanton, Ph.D.
Executive Director, Mid-South Association of
Independent Schools (MAIS), Jackson, MS

"Understanding and realizing the intricacies and importance of good governance is critical for the success of any school head, and Dr. Bill Mott captures this unique and vital piece of independent school life exceptionally well. I highly recommend any school leader or aspiring leader to read *Healthy Boards, Successful Schools*—it will be time well invested. Good school governance resides in the successful relationship between the board and the school head. Understanding the intricacies and realizing the importance of such a working relationship is vital for the school community. Dr. Mott captures this unique piece of independent school life incredibly well and in full, vivid, 'real life' stories. Any school leader will benefit greatly from reading this book and learning the valuable lessons it provides."

Patrick Roberts
Head of School, Palmer Trinity School, Miami, FL

"Among the voices in governance and leadership in independent schools, Bill Mott's is one of the biggest and most compelling. He demystifies the complex relationship between boards and heads and fosters a deep passion for fulfilling the school's mission. Every head and every trustee should keep Bill's books handy."

Damian Kavanagh, Ed.S., CAE
Executive Director, MISBO (Mid-South Independent School Business Officers), Atlanta, GA

"If you're serious about serving on an independent school board, you need to read *Healthy Boards, Successful Schools*. Bill Mott tackles the key issues facing heads of schools and independent school boards. He captures the essence of what it means to be a great board member and identifies the prime ingredients needed to create and sustain a strong, healthy relationship between the board and head. This is a must-read for every board member."

Paul Brenner
Head of School, Wayne Christian School, Goldsboro, NC

"Bill Mott's book is a clear and comprehensive guide to the relationship between the school head and the board. It is truly thorough in its coverage of all critical areas of governance. If you want to make a difference as a school head, then share this book with your board today! True insight for new as well as established heads. Thanks, Bill, for writing *Healthy Boards, Successful Schools*!"

Carl "Chuck" Sabo
Former Head of School, St. Bernard Academy, Nashville, TN

"Dr. William Mott's latest book is the quintessential resource board of trustees and heads of school at private, independent, and faith-based schools. His comprehensive range of topics coupled with his experienced perspective into the interactions and relationships among the board of trustees and the head of school provide the essential framework to cultivate healthy board/head relationships—successively building healthy schools."

Jon Shoulders
President, Friendship Christian School, Lebanon, TN

HEALTHY BOARDS

---◆---

SUCCESSFUL SCHOOLS

The Impact of Governance and Leadership
on Independent and Faith-Based Schools

WILLIAM R. MOTT, PH.D.

Publisher's Note: Some of the material in this book also appeared in the author's previous works, *The Board Game* and *Super Boards*. For purposes of this book, some material from the other titles has been revised and repurposed to conform to the unique circumstances of independent and faith-based schools.

Cover design by LA Creative (www.lacreative09.com)

Author photo by Joe Strickland

ISBN: 979-8-9871314-1-1

For Courtney Mott
Love of my life and best friend

and

Edith Whitehead Mott
Loving, supportive, encouraging mother

CONTENTS

Chapter One
HEALTHY BOARDS, SUCCESSFUL SCHOOLS: ONE
BOARD—ONE VOICE..11
The relationship between healthy governing boards and healthy independent and faith-based schools is all too often a metric overlooked by those in leadership positions. However, the success of schools is directly related to the relationship of the board and the head of school. How can trustees better serve, better understand their roles and responsibilities?

CASE STORY #1: What does the finance committee
understand about school finance or financial assistance? 25
How are standing committees selected and what assumptions are made regarding their knowledge of a particular area, such as finance? Being a good businessman or businesswoman, it

doesn't necessarily mean he or she understands school finance and the manner in which the budget is created. Trustees occasionally believe what applies to one school automatically applies to another school. That can lead to some unfortunate conversations.

The search for a new head of school is an enormous responsibility for the board of trustees fundamental to its role. The process calls for a series of strategic steps to give the best possible chance for finding and securing the leader who is the right fit for the school. Engaging a firm to assist in the search process or learning what is involved will enable the board to successfully complete this task. One of the critical areas to understand is what happens when the search process includes an internal candidate who is a well-respected leader in the school community.

Recruiting board members is an intentional and thoughtful undertaking that takes place in an environment conducive to engaging in a discussion that represents the serious nature of what is at stake. Perhaps someone's front yard where you are admiring her flowers is not exactly the venue that will yield the best possible candidate.

In many schools several board members typically, or often, join the board at a specified time of the year, thus creating a "class" of new board members that begins and potentially is re-elected or rotates off at the same time.

The transition that leads from one board chair to the next can result in unintended consequences. Does the new board chair have a different set of expectations than the previous chair? How do these shifting expectations impact the head? This is a defining moment for a school wishing to reach a new level of maturity.

The independent school governing board of trustees is critical to the effective operation—not because the board has the day-to-day oversight but rather because of its fiduciary, mission, vision, and strategic direction responsibilities.

Trustees who intimidate in order to achieve their goals may be rare but not as rare as we think. What happens when a trustee believes that the way he or she views the future of the school is the best way to move forward? If visioning and strategic direction mean something, what happens when an opportunity is presented that had not been considered previously? If process is important, what circumstances allow for the board to vote by e-mail?

Independent school board chairs are in a position to have enormous influence over the school, the board, and the head of school. The underlying theme for this person is to have the best possible relationship with the head of school. That is the pretext for the chair's five most important responsibilities.

While the board chair may not always agree with the head on operational matters, he or she should provide a level of support that indicates a certain acceptance not to entertain an issue that involves student discipline. How does the head feel about the nature of their relationship when the board gives an audience to a parent when the head of school has already taken action and resolved the matter?

How and why a board carries out its responsibilities in the manner it does will define what is valued. Behavior, attitude, beliefs, philosophy, traditions, and how the board and head of school work together will define culture.

The board appoints a new head of school and almost immediately there are problems. The chair of the board and search committee have all left the board—almost immediately after the new head's appointment. The board sees it as unnecessary to conduct a retreat to get acquainted with the new head. And to top it all off, the new head is following the founding head who has been in that role for over 30 years. What could possibly go wrong? Then a trustee decides to have his spouse apply for a staff position at the school. What could go wrong indeed!

A faculty member reaches out directly to the new board chair. The chair, uncertain of her role, responds in a way that challenges the authority of the head of school. What issues are the responsibility of the board what are those that are not? The new board chair finds herself on a slippery slope. Is there a way to salvage this mess? Michael may have the answers the new chair is anxious to learn.

Chapter Ten
The committee on trustees and others on the board who have a responsibility to secure new members of the board should consider seven key characteristics before securing new board members. These characteristics will help define the board's qualities, experience, and expertise.

Board chairs and the school's committee on trustees are in positions of leadership and responsibility when it comes to selecting new trustees. The best boards include members who are involved and listen to the opinions expressed by the head. Collaboration is a key factor in developing a great list of prospective trustees.

Chapter Eleven
There are numerous ways for a board to be structured. Many of these unique ways can be found in the language of the bylaws and policies. In order to achieve greatness for the school, what is the best structure and what best practice should be followed?

Occasionally the board is confused about what role, if any, it should play in setting financial aid policy or what knowledge the finance committee or other trustees should have about specific families that receive financial assistance based on demonstrated need. Is this an area of overstepping into school operations or a legitimate board policy issue?

Chapter Twelve
Perhaps the task of an independent school board that is most often misunderstood or neglected in the recruitment process is that of fundraising on behalf of the school. It is not simply a necessity; it must be a fundamental responsibility and therefore a priority for each board member.

Chapter Thirteen
The fiduciary responsibility for the board of trustees is fundamental to sustaining the school well into the future. What role does planned giving play in assuring the school's financial security, and how can the board facilitate a strategy for success?

Chapter Fourteen
A board often overlooks its role as school ambassador and its responsibility to play a strategic role in supporting the school's admissions and marketing efforts.

Best practices would suggest that the board chair and the administrative officer have fairly limited contact and that any communication be filtered through the head of school. This is considered to be a best practice because the board (and the board chair) has one employee—the head of school. What happens when this breaks down? Why is it that when this best practice is put to the test trustees, more often than not, fail the test? The consequences can be devastating!

Chapter Fifteen
THE CONNECTION BETWEEN SUPPORTIVE
School growth may not be the number one priority of every independent and faith-based school, but many recognize that a strong enrollment and enhanced programs point to viability, forward progress, and sustainability. How does any of this relate to the effectiveness and success of the board? Is there a connection between school growth and a high-functioning board?

From a governance perspective, there is no need for a board chair to communicate with individual members of the school's administrative staff—especially if seeking to discover any issues or concerns about the head of school. Such a scenario raises three critical issues. First, the chair should never go to a staff member to find out anything regarding the head. Second, as an individual, the board chair has no authority when communicating with staff. And third, such behavior demonstrates a complete lack of support and trust for the head.

another school, that board member should step down. The principle is that if a trustee—someone closest to the inner workings of the school—moves their children to another school, it signals other parents that perhaps there is something wrong. It begins a guessing game and is a distraction. What happens when the trustee refuses to step down?

The Governance Promise is comprised of six statements that speak directly to attitude, behavior, and reflection about the work of the board. Why are these principles important and what do they say about the board, their work, and their relationship to the head of school?

What is involved in evaluating the head of school? What happens when a board chair enters the picture with very different criteria to evaluate the head? Should power be concentrated in one person to the extent that they are allowed to hold two different offices on the board at the same time? Evaluations are a helpful and useful way to advance the school. But there are ways they can be effective tools and ways they can be misused and harmful.

Chapter Twenty-One

There is something genuine and fundamental and which brings that element of authenticity when you are asked to sign a document signifying and establishing an agreement, or covenant, between and among the board and school.

Extreme personalities suggest putting ideology before what
is best for the school—and those who strive to lead them.
The result of working with the board chair who has hired the
head and the next board chair may lead to being terminated.
Moderation coupled with a desire to set aside personal
agendas will place the school before self-interest. The board
chair should always seek ways to work with the head—even if
they may mean setting aside some of his or her own particular
desires.

Chapter Twenty-Two
*The head of school has a complex job with many moving parts. It
is a position of enormous responsibility and filled with challenges,
opportunities, great joy, and some frustration. It is often said
that unless you are or have been a head of school, it is difficult to
accurately understand what this person experiences.*

The head of school and associate head for business are
ambushed at a board retreat when a trustee and former head of
school asks a question that creates significant division between
the school's leadership and the trustees. Institutional memory
plays a key role in understanding past policies and current
circumstances. Candor and trust take a back seat in this story
regarding accounts receivable.

Chapter Twenty-Three
*The process and method of evaluating the head of school is an
important responsibility of the board. The board must work with*

the head to develop a meaningful procedure that results in an evaluation that is truly beneficial to both parties.

Partnership, collaboration, shared vision and other similar characteristics should define the working relationship between the head of school, board chair, and board members. However, what happens when one or a few members of the board are firmly convinced that not only does the head report to the board (and each trustee) but that the head should understand that he or she is required to do what the board wants? What kind of culture can this school have when attitudes like this prevail? Is this a healthy environment for a head and board as they attempt to work together?

Chapter Twenty-Four
The director of advancement has a unique relationship with the governing board. Because both fundraising and the marketing are critical to a school's ability and opportunity to fulfill its mission, the person in this role needs to work closely with the entire board.

The development committee is a very important standing committee of the school's board. As such, the chair of the development committee must work closely with the head and director of development (chief development officer). Trust, respect, and support are characteristics that are essential for this relationship to thrive and to yield the best results for the school.

Chapter Twenty-Five

While not a formal part of the governance structure, the introduction of some type of advisory board can be beneficial to the school as well as a type of observable "training ground" for prospective trustees. However, for such groups to be successful, the head must recognize the most effective way to create and sustain an advisory board and devote the time necessary for it to thrive.

CASE STORY #24: Demonstrating unwavering support for the head...266
Throughout this book, it has been shown again and again that the relationship between the head of school, the board chair, and the board of trustees is the single biggest contributor to the success and viability of the school. Is there a way for the board chair and board to tangibly demonstrate their support? Heads thrive in an environment in which they believe they have the full support of the board.

    10. Attitude Is Everything
    9. Finding Balance from the Board
    8. Board Members with an Agenda

Author's Note
Regarding Terminology

I recognize and understand that independent schools, faith-based schools, and private schools of every kind utilize different terminology to describe their governing boards. For the sake clarity and continuity, I have chosen to use the term *board of trustees* to describe the governing boards referenced throughout this book. Also, independent schools, faith-based schools, and private schools have different titles for a school's CEO. Again, for the sake of continuity, I have decided to use the term *head of school* to describe the individuals in this position.

In addition, I also recognize that there are numerous faith-based schools that have a church or denominational affiliation and that such an affiliation often results in a modification to the governance structure presented in this book. I have not attempted to address these different structures other than to acknowledge their existence.

FOREWORD

Dr. Jeff Jackson

"The single biggest way to impact an organization
is to focus on leadership development.
There is almost no limit to the potential of
an organization that recruits good people,
raises them up as leaders
and continually develops them."
—*John C. Maxwell*

T o understand independent school leadership is to understand school governance and ultimately to understand the impact of healthy boards. Dr. Bill Mott is keenly aware of the relationship between "healthy boards" and "successful schools " as evidenced in this must-read book.

During my career as a head of school in both Louisiana and Georgia, as Assistant Professor at Palm Beach Atlantic University, Adjunct Professor at Mercer University, and currently as President of the Georgia Independent School Association (GISA), I have had the opportunity to work with a variety of school, church, and business leaders, and most recently as GISA implemented the Emerging Leaders Institute. In some instances, I have encountered leaders who lacked knowledge when dealing with the complex issues of boards and school governance. Board selection, retention, and responsibilities require a depth of knowledge and understanding that many merely gain by chance as they travel their leadership journey.

As a result of years of experience and research gained from independent school leadership and board service, Dr. Mott is recognized as a foremost leader in the world of independent school governance. I confidently use this book as a reference guide while instructing aspiring leaders and training heads and boards in the areas of school governance. It is an ideal textbook with clear and practical case studies. For boards and heads who care deeply about the missions of their schools and those who desire to see them succeed, Dr. Mott's outstanding book is essential. He shares wisdom and experiences in a classic, common sense, easy-to-follow manner. By studying his words and applying his guiding concepts, independent school leaders and boards will be strengthened and enhanced, resulting in the ultimate goal of *Healthy Boards, Successful Schools.*

Jeff Jackson, MBA, Ed.D.
President, Georgia Independent School Association (GISA)

Prologue

◆

Lessons Learned: A Story About Making a Difference and Deciding Which Stonecutter You Will Be

In 1666 the Great Fire of London severely damaged one of London's most iconic landmarks, St. Paul's Cathedral. King Charles II commissioned the renowned architect Sir Christopher Wren to rebuild the enormous structure, and construction finally began in 1675. One day as the great architect was walking through the construction site he encountered many stonecutters. Wren approached one of the men and asked, "What are you working on?" The stonecutter, perhaps not aware of to whom he was speaking, said, "I'm cutting stone—what does it look like I'm doing?" In other words, "Isn't it obvious?" Wren shook his head and moved on.

As he continued his survey of the site he spoke with another stonecutter and posed the same question. This man looked at the legendary architect and replied, "I'm working with you to build the greatest cathedral on earth." Wren thanked the man for his vision and passion for the work he was doing. Wren recognized that a positive attitude coupled with the skills needed to carry out the stonecutter's task resulted in the stone cutter seeing his role as contributing to something greater than himself.

This is a favorite story of mine. As I was writing this book, I thought it conveyed three valuable lessons regarding the nature of leadership and how that leadership makes such a mark on everyone connected with the leader and the school.

The first of the three lessons has to do with shared vision. This unique story acknowledges the value of working together for a purpose greater than yourself. The second of the two stonecutters understood his role—that he was a part of something very important. He shared Christopher Wren's vision for doing something extraordinary. And being part of something extraordinary was a life-changing experience.

The second lesson contained in this story tells us something about attitude adjustment. Thomas Jefferson said, "Nothing can stop someone with the right attitude from achieving their goal; and nothing on earth can help someone with the wrong attitude." Clearly, stonecutter number one had an attitude problem! How you approach a task, the way you feel about yourself and those around you, can dramatically impact your success in achieving your goals. *Your attitude significantly defines who you are.* The first stonecutter Wren spoke with might have had the same skill level as the second stonecutter. However, without the passion, commitment, and dedication to participate in something exceptional like the rebuilding of St. Paul's, he would not be as fulfilled as the second cutter.

The third lesson has everything to do with the recognition that making a difference has much to do with self-awareness, understanding that we individually and collectively can make a positive impact. The second stonecutter knew full well his skills were going to make a difference on the appearance and strength of the cathedral. Making a difference goes to the very core of who we are and what we try to instill. Understanding that you are blessed and therefore bear some responsibility for stepping into the gap is filled with the idea that making a positive difference is worthy of our best.

The value and significance of working together to achieve something incredibly important, having the most positive attitude possible, and the idea that you can make a difference and impact those around you, all resonate with the underlying theme of why it is essential for independent and faith-based schools to seek, to serve, to lead, and to inspire.

So, the question for each school leader, each head of school, and each trustee is, "Which stonecutter will you decide to be?"

Introduction

◆

Inspired Leadership and the Spirit of Collaboration

"My words fly up, my thoughts remain below:
Words without thoughts never to heaven go."
—*From* Hamlet *by William Shakespeare*

Uniformity and unity. What do these two words mean, and what do they have to do with the leadership and governance relationships that are so critical to the belief that healthy boards and healthy schools have the most positive influence on independent and faith-based schools? Uniformity suggests that there is value in sameness and that differences are not appreciated. On the other hand, unity suggests a level of togetherness as in the concept that we are all in this together. While I sense a genuine and meaningful difference between the two, I can see that these two concepts can be misinterpreted. My concern is that too many who labor or volunteer in the world of independent and faith-based schools have confused the two and shy away from unity for fear it will be seen as uniformity. Governing boards at independent and faith-based schools will, all too often, perceive this as a sign of weakness. Uniformity should be a concern. Unity should not. Somewhere along the way boards have taken on the personality and culture that it is a sign of strength to be at odds with one another or with the head of school or with some operational aspect of the school.

In reality, there is enormous strength in unity. Differences of opinion and sometimes philosophy are healthy and occasionally necessary for schools to thrive. However, too many boards have come to lean heavily on this idea instead of discovering the real strength that is required in putting self-interests and agendas aside and working for what is in the best interest of the school. History and culture coupled with egos and a misplaced emphasis on individuality have led schools to the brink of disaster. It is time to step back and reflect on where we are, what we are doing, and where we are headed. Heads of school who somehow allow themselves to be harassed and manipulated by strong individuals on the board and board chairs themselves will not be able to thrive nor even survive in such circumstances.

Are there excellent governing boards? Yes! Are there excellent heads of school? Yes! Are there many schools in which this relationship prospers leading to the success of the school? Absolutely! However, what works today may or may not work tomorrow. Independent and faith-based schools operate in a climate of constant change and ongoing challenges. One constant, though, should be the healthiest possible board and school leadership. It is the single most important factor in determining the health of the school.

Independent and faith-based schools have always faced both unique challenges and amazing opportunities as they seek to live out their mission and vision. These challenges and opportunities continue and arguably are more acute than ever before, especially when you consider economic factors that have certainly placed stress on many schools. All the while, incredible people work hard to lead these schools with passion, commitment, and a renewed dedication to their profession. Where in this panorama of challenges and opportunities do we find the board of trustees? That is the central question for us to discover in this book. It is their leadership and spirit of collaboration that we are seeking.

Many books address the topic of school governance and board development, but taking a fresh look at the subject from a different perspective is often necessary. Perspective is an interesting vantage point. Having served as both a head of school and a trustee at several independent schools gives me a unique perspective to bring to this discussion.

With this book, I have tried to achieve something different— to focus attention on several issues that serve to reveal and distinguish independent and faith-based schools that have strong, dynamic boards that include leaders whose genuine purpose is to be the best possible board member. The seven specific objectives include:

1. To demonstrate that the correlation between healthy boards and successful schools is the determining factor between thriving and surviving.
2. To describe and discuss the transformational responsibilities of the board of trustees, including the committee on trustees, that elevate their mission to recruit, retain, educate, and evaluate the board.
3. To introduce a component to the discussion of board responsibilities that solidifies the all-important relationship that board members must have with one another and with the school's leadership. This Covenant Agreement is a document that some schools have adopted but do not properly utilize or simply see as having little value.

4. To think differently and more openly about governance and to create a culture that understands that serving on the board is serious work, but that hard work pays off when you joyfully experience excellence—the capstone of the experience.

5. To assure board chairs and heads of schools that your current circumstances do not define where they are going, only where they are. A school's, and specifically a board's, ability to function at the highest level can move from bad to good and from good to great. It is possible and worth the effort (perhaps the sacrifices) required to move forward.

6. To reinforce the central theme that although the board of trustees of an independent school consists of many individuals, once a decision is made, it must recognize the value of unity, one voice, one vision!

7. To introduce to the board culture the value and importance of striving for best practices and how they indicate that the board and head are ever moving forward recognizing the vital concept that improvement comes only by changing and evolving. It is, after all, the students and their experience that will define the impact of the school.

As referenced above with the quotation from Shakespeare, this book is to be thoughtful and intentional in its approach to the topic of how independent school governing boards can genuinely strive to be excellent in carrying out their tasks and responsibilities. Words alone are not enough—but the right words, coupled with the right actions, will make a positive difference and have the greatest influence.

Leadership is defined in different ways by different people with different perspectives. Here is a partial definition that fits the theme of this book: *Leadership is the ability of someone or a group to encourage and to inspire others. It is the ability to discover the best in someone and, through encouragement and inspiration, to bring out the best in individuals or groups. It is the recognition that relationships matter, particularly the relationship between the head of school and the board of trustees. The ability to articulate a vision and connect that with a timetable is what separates great leaders from all others.* Through this lens we shine a spotlight on creating and sustaining healthy boards and, ultimately, healthy schools. Independent schools face many uncertainties and numerous challenges across the educational spectrum. But there is one certainty that is valid; the correlation between healthy boards and successful schools is undeniable.

Educators and governing boards have enormous importance because of the mission of preparing the next generation of leaders who will lead by serving, who will lead by making a difference, and who will lead by those who have influenced their lives. The ultimate objective of this book is raising awareness of the issues and engaging in meaningful discussion. That is where the magic may be found. It is difficult for the board to work toward innovation without the knowledge of understanding how it impacts a board and a school's success. My hope is that you will discover the power and value of unity in an environment where working toward a shared vision is a sincere and valid show of strength.

Chapter One

◆

Healthy Boards,
Successful Schools:
One Board—One Voice

The impact that independent and faith-based school governing boards have on the schools they serve cannot be overstated. The theme of this book is the direct correlation and connection healthy boards have with the health and sustainability of schools. This topic and the issues presented continue to be discussed and debated, but the evidence is clear and compelling. The most important factor that determines the success of the school is the undeniable relationship between the board, the board chair, and the head of school. The central question then becomes how do we get this right and what necessary steps will ensure that what we have created is sustainable? The most direct path to living out the school's mission and vision is the recognition that for schools to be at their healthiest, the board must be at its healthiest with a complete understanding, acceptance, and implementation of its appropriate role and impact on the school.

Primary Responsibilities of the Board

The board of trustees has numerous responsibilities and all will be explored. There are three that are fundamental to their role. In the case of these three, and perhaps all responsibilities, they cannot be delegated to other groups or individuals. A board may receive input, support, and encouragement in certain aspects of their work. But, in the end, the board must accept that these specific responsibilities are theirs and theirs alone.

Establish the Mission

Most boards and schools understand and embrace the compelling truth that its mission defines a school's identity and purpose through character, culture, and programs. The manner in which the mission is articulated, communicated, utilized, and referred to say much about the level of institutional effectiveness. If trustees don't know the mission statement word for word, they should have the ability to state the central message in their own words. The ability to do so conveys they comprehend the central message of its meaning.

Independent and faith-based school mission statements may appear vague or, in some cases, generic, thus giving the impression that these institutions are passing the same one around. It would be more accurate to say that mission statements are intentionally imprecise, allowing schools and the leadership teams certain latitude in interpreting direction and strategy without having to continually modify the statement.

Crafting the wording of a mission statement often includes the work of a board committee charged with reviewing the statement. This is usually done in an environment in which the board is embarking on a strategic planning process or perhaps revising the school's bylaws. This committee prepares a draft of the statement and makes a recommendation to the board. The board then will review and ratify or possibly revise the statement. But the mission statement is one that can only be amended or be completely rewritten by the board of trustees.

Accepting Fiduciary Responsibility

The second of the board's three fundamental responsibilities is sustaining the school's financial health. The simple and undeniable truth is that without adequate financial resources to operate the school, the mission will be irrelevant—no money, no mission. It is imperative that the board fully understands the school's financial model. Budgeting, financial statements, balance sheets, endowment creation and growth, capital projects are all under the scrutiny of the board. The head and school CFO play a vital role in preparing, maintaining, and communicating financial issues, but the board must approve the budget, manage the endowment, and determine the need for any major capital initiative.

Hire and Value the Head of School

The third fundamental responsibility of the board is to hire the head of school, partner to ensure this person's success, and make a change only when it is deemed undeniably necessary to do so. The terminology that all too often comes with this responsibility is to "hire and fire the head." This way of describing the relationship between the board and head is problematic and lacks the recognition that the achievement of a positive relationship is essential to the school's capacity for success. Partnership is crucial.

It is essential that the board and head see their respective roles as one in which they work together for what is in the best interest of the school. From the perspective of the school's hierarchy, the head accepts that the board has appointed him or her and the board understands the reporting and evaluation relationship that comes with this position. But, in the end, the school will thrive when the board and head partner with one another to accomplish something genuinely special, the success of its students.

Experience and history tell us that all too often the board does not understand its role and acts and reacts without fully recognizing the consequences of making a change in leadership. They fail to appreciate the challenging role of the head and act with haste and without recognizing the impact this action will have on the school. There are times when the fit is not right and circumstances where the head is carrying duties that may not be in the best interest of the school. However, there are many occasions in which a few members of the board have a conflict with the head, so they encourage, and sometimes intimidate, other board members to see issues their way. The board must step back from the edge and make informed decisions about what actions are truly in the best interest of the school. Is there a legitimate concern? Does the board fully appreciate its role in this circumstance? Is the board willing to engage in best practices? Does the head need to resign or would the school be better served by removing one or more members of the board? These questions and others must be addressed before a terrible and far-reaching mistake is made that will have significant consequences for the school.

The Board Functioning as a Team

The manner in which these board responsibilities are executed determines the difference between boards that are healthy and those that are detrimental to the school's future. How then should healthy boards view their function as a team, working together to guarantee as much as possible for the sustainability of the school? There are eleven areas of responsibility that determine this:

1. Working together to develop the mission and vision statements, and to determine if the head is following and leading from the intent of these statements.

2. Develop the strategic plan and monitor key indicators of performance to ensure the plan is being implemented in accordance with the timetable established in the plan.

3. Focus discussions on strategic issues rather than tactical or operational ones. The board's role is one of viability— looking at the school's future and creating the path that leads the school in the right direction.

4. Create and maintain an effective committee structure. There are two issues that help guide the board to a sustainable committee model. First, the size of the board influences what the committee structure looks like including how many and how big committees are formed. The larger the board, the greater the potential to have either more committees or more on the committees. A smaller board may mean fewer committees or, in some cases, the board being a "committee of the whole." Second, the bylaws should spell out the number, size, scope, and which standing committees the board must have. Also, unless the bylaws stipulate otherwise, non-board members may also serve on board committees.

5. The board's committee on trustees (also known as the governance committee) has the responsibility to recruit trustees who can distinguish their roles as parents, or grandparents, or alumni from their role as members of the board. This can dramatically reduce confusion regarding the board's legitimate strategic role versus its improper operational role.

6. Plan and implement an effective orientation or onboarding program. New board members will already

have some familiarity with the work of the board if clear expectations and duties were presented during the recruitment process. An orientation program will go much further by ensuring that when the time comes to attend their first meeting, each new board member will "be up to speed" and prepared to be a contributing member of the board. In addition to this onboarding session, the committee should also consider a mentoring program by connecting new board members with their experienced counterparts. This is another relational and communication path that will enrich their time of service on the board.

7. Apply or develop a methodology and process, perhaps with the committee on trustees taking the lead, by which the board can be evaluated successfully. The board's willingness to evaluate their performance is a hit and miss proposition. Many boards value the process and recognize that such a process is designed to enhance their ability to effectively serve the board and serve the school. Elsewhere in this book is an evaluation template any independent or faith-based school could adopt or modify to better fit their unique circumstances. Following the completion of an evaluation questionnaire, it is the responsibility of the board to come together in a retreat setting to review, analyze, and take the appropriate action based on the results. The committee on trustees can then monitor the manner in which the board implements those areas that require attention.

8. The board must never function as a court of appeal regarding any operational aspect of the school. Disciplinary issues, dress code, admissions related issues, cheerleader selection process, who is cast in the

play and who is not, the look of the school uniform, and the list goes on. A highly qualified and professional faculty, staff, and ultimately the head of school make all of these decisions. A board member may not agree with the process or decision, but operational decisions are not theirs to make. At the end of the day the question that needs to be addressed is: Was the process followed as described in the handbook? It is the reason why school officials have handbooks—to provide guidance, policies, and a process that are in the best interest of the school—and bring clarity and purpose to a particular issue.

9. At many independent and faith-based schools the governing board is comprised of current parents as well as other constituencies. The consequences of this are both enormously positive and occasionally a difficult governance challenge. In fact, one of the most significant challenges for schools comes from parents who are also trustees and their lack of knowledge concerning how to effectively communicate with other parents of the school. In terms of responsibilities board members who are also parents should not engage in conversations (verbal, text, e-mail, social media, etc.) with other parents regarding issues that do not relate to the work of the board. Always direct these parents to where the issue can best be resolved—faculty, staff, coach, or head of school.

10. Board members, from time to time, will be under the impression that as parent, or grandparent, or alumnus of the school they believe it is their job to represent that particular constituency. This idea or belief is false. No member of the board is a spokesperson nor do they give voice to what they believe others in that constituency want to hear

or put forth as an agenda. Board members are elected to the board by other members (that is, a self-perpetuating board) because of the skills, knowledge, expertise, connections, and wisdom they bring to enrich the work of this group. Board members have been heard to say, "As a parent, I believe my job as a board member is to listen to their concerns and be their voice." This is not the case and should not be encouraged.

11. One of the most vital characteristics and components of an independent school governing board is the concept that outside the boardroom, it is always preferable to speak with one voice. This is a critical aspect of the school and should not be confused with board's ability and desire to discuss, debate, and disagree on the critical issues and challenges faced by the school at any given point in its life. What is equally critical is the board functioning as a team, being of one accord when communicating about board actions. In the life cycle of a board, a range of issues must be addressed, and the content and discussion of issues must remain confidential.

Conduct of Individual Board Members

In addition to the collective roles and responsibilities of the board of trustees is the recognition that individual behavior and action may have profound consequences to the individual, the entire board of trustees, and ultimately, the school. How then should the conduct of individual board members contribute to the healthiest possible boards?

- Each member of the board must always **demonstrate the highest standards of integrity, character, and ethical behavior.** In other words, they should share the values that are most likely upheld by the school. This point may seem to be obvious, and perhaps for most schools that is the case. However, the board should not dismiss this by assuming it is always true. Making this a characteristic and a condition on the selection of trustees reinforces the idea that values matter and that the board and the school are guided by ideals and principles that are non-negotiable.

- To the extent possible, a board and board members must **avoid conflicts of interest.** This concept should be understood by the committee on trustees and explained to each prospective member of the board. For many schools, a statement regarding conflict of interest is included in the school's bylaws. Included here is a sample opening declaration. The complete statement is found in Appendix C.

> The board of trustees affirms that the trustees, officers, administrators, faculty and other employees of (school) have an obligation to exercise their authority and to carry out the duties of their respective positions for the sole benefit of (school). They should avoid placing themselves in positions in which their personal interests are, or may be, in conflict with the interests of (school). Where a potential conflict of interest exists, it shall be the responsibility of the person involved or any other person with knowledge to notify the board of trustees of the circumstances resulting in the potential conflict so that the board of trustees can provide such guidance and take such action as it shall deem appropriate.

This is one of the numerous reasons why the trustee screening process is essential to ensuring that the committee on trustees builds the best board possible.

- During their time of service on the board, each board member should be required to accept their critical role as financial contributors to the school and to engage in supporting fundraising activities and events of the school. How is this communicated to a prospective board member? The committee on trustees, the board chair, and the head of school all bear some responsibility to make clear the board's vision and intentions in this critical area of responsibility. When trustees demonstrate strong financial support for the school, they send a clear signal that the constituency possibly closest to the school (board of trustees) recognizes its role regarding the sustainability of the school.

- One area of board responsibility often overlooked has to do with members **serving as ambassadors and advocates for the school**. Each member has a sphere of influence that they can draw upon to build awareness and support. Therefore, trustees should be conversant about programs and marketing initiatives. You simply never know when an opportunity will emerge to make the most of circumstances beneficial to the school. The key to making this work is for board members to be aware that this is an area where they are in a unique position to make a positive difference. Too many independent and faith-based school boards fail to recognize the significance of their influence or haven't been told how much of a priority this is.

- **Attendance at board and committee meetings** should be understood, but all too often board members allow themselves permission to miss meetings with alarming frequency. During the trustee recruitment process, it should be made clear that attendance while not mandatory (we are talking about volunteers) is strongly encouraged. This should be a part of the board culture with a process in place to remind board members of the importance of this. What about attendance at school events? Certainly, it is easy for a trustee parent to attend events that involve their children. Occasionally the chair of the board or head of school will suggest when the presence of board members is needed. When this happens, trustees should make an effort to attend such events.

- Board members must understand **the importance of speaking with one voice when outside the boardroom.** This best practice coupled with adhering to the principle of confidentiality will increase the health of both the board and school. Discussions and disagreements within the confines of the board room are healthy as well. But, in the end, a united front behind decisions made and the leadership of the school will suggest to the school's constituencies a sense of confidence, trust, and support for actions taken by the board.

- We live in a time of increased scrutiny, accountability, and sensitivity to actions and inappropriate and harmful behavior to students, teachers, parents, and others. Not only are such behaviors detrimental to the individuals involved, they are also harmful to the school. **Awareness of even the possibility of such behavior by a board member requires a response.** If there is something that doesn't seem right, share such concerns with the board chair and head of school. These two individuals cannot be expected to know everything going on. Do not assume knowledge when the situation may involve physical or emotional harm to anyone.

A Healthy Relationship with the Head of School

The school's board of trustees also has very specific responsibilities when it comes to their treatment and relationship with the head of school. Again, adherence to these best practices will do much to foster this relationship and provide the head and the board with confidence, support, and encouragement. What should every trustee know about this relationship?

- The school's board has one employee—the head of school. The head directly and indirectly has final authority when it comes to all personnel matters. If the head chooses, he or she may include the board chair or other board members in certain specific personnel discussions and decisions. However, without exception, the head of school is the only employee of the board of trustees. While most trustees accept this principle, there are times when this is not followed and the board believes it is their prerogative to interject thoughts, feelings, ideas, and biases into personnel matters. This will inevitably lead to trouble. And if a trustee has a spouse, friend, relative, or other acquaintance he or she wishes to put forward for a position at the school, that trustee must remove himself or herself from any involvement in the decision and may need to step down from the board. The potential for a conflict of interest is enormous and extremely damaging.

- The process that the board establishes to evaluate the work of the head of school speaks volumes about the relationship between the board and the head. When it comes to this evaluation, this is an area where the concept of partnership comes into play. The board, or more specifically, the committee on the head, should work with the head to establish the criteria by which the head is evaluated. Two factors potentially come into play:

1. The committee and the head develop goals that are relevant to a specific academic year. The head outlines the goals that he or she believe are the most important for a particular year based on circumstances that relate to this time.

2. The committee on the head and head have agreed upon criteria that refer to specific metrics that occur every year. These typically have to do with budget, tuition, fundraising, enrollment, retention, and other mutually agreed upon measurements for success.

- Supporting and partnering with the head is much more than simply lip service about support; it is a genuine methodology having to do with the manner in which the board treats the head. There is a distinct difference between talking about respect and actually demonstrating this trait. The board chair should insist that the head never be treated in any way other than with complete support, respect, and encouragement.

- Since the board has only one employee, all management and administrative functions are the responsibility of the head of school. Therefore, functions like the development and implementation of the school's organizational chart are the charge of the head. This is clearly an area in which the head determines what he or she believes works best for the school. The head may seek input from others (including other heads) but rarely will trustees have insight into this issue. It is not necessarily true that a business model or for-profit organization will relate to the effectiveness or efficiency of an independent school. The board chair may need to remind board members not to meddle but to trust the head and his or her ability to manage and lead the school.

- One of the most misunderstood aspects of the relationship between the school's board and the head has to do with the fact that the head reports to the board and not to individual trustees. To be fair, trustees, for the most part, do not realize how this works and will not understand the impact this has on the head. However, neither ignorance or arrogance is a legitimate reason for such behavior. The head cannot be expected to address issues individual trustees have with the school. And the majority of these issues do not relate to the work of the board but rather to concerns or issue with a teacher, coach, or another staff member. Or the trustee is trying to resolve an issue a parent has. These are not legitimate reasons to individually seek out the head for a one-on-one conversation. Also, it is critical that a board member never treat the head as someone who works for them. Corporate executives and CEOs will from time to time believe that the head of school is one of his or her employees and answer to them. The committee on trustees must clarify this and ensure that a prospective trustee understand that the head does not answer to individual trustees. The head works closely with the chair and with committees. Board members must never use their position as trustees to expect special treatment or favors.

Indeed, there is a compelling case to be made that the stronger and healthier the board, the more clarity they have in understanding their role and how it differs from the school's administration; the stronger the board, the stronger, healthier, and more successful the school. If this correlation and assertion is valid then it becomes an institutional imperative that boards act accordingly and move forward now knowing what best practices look like, how they should work together, relate to the head of school, and what is in the best interest of the school. The stakes are too high to do otherwise.

CASE STORY #1

What Does the Finance Committee Understand About School Finance or Financial Assistance?

Many independent and faith-based schools provide tuition or financial assistance to families that qualify for that type of support. Typically, a third-party organization reviews family financial information and makes a determination and recommendation on the amount the family can pay based on the information provided. Schools, in turn, based on their policy or other factors, such as an amount set aside in their budget, will award families financial assistance. In addition, there is a growing trend among schools to communicate or market this in such a way that it is described as variable tuition—tuition based on a family's ability to pay. It is not uncommon for schools to utilize assistance as an enrollment management strategy and a recognition of what an economically diverse population can bring to the school.

For many independent schools, depending on the state in which they are located, there is another factor that must be considered. For these schools that provide high school (varsity) athletics there is the issue of how much need-based aid can be provided to student athletes, and how that impacts the school's overall budget. The question then becomes, how much does the board's finance committee know about or understand these two separate but related issues? And, could their lack of knowledge impact the way in which the full board comprehends what this means for the budget?

For many years Lawrence Academy had participated in a comprehensive program of varsity athletics. The school competed in the state's private school division, which meant that Lawrence could provide need-based assistance to student athletes. However, the policy of the state association stipulated that schools in the private school division must limit the aid they provide to only the amount the family qualified for—which many schools adopted as an internal policy. Schools that were not in the private school division could not offer any financial assistance regardless of a family's financial circumstances. This issue, whether or not the school participated in the private school division, had a significant impact on the school's financial aid budget. The difference at such schools would be dramatic.

Jim, and his firm, had been the school's auditor for a number of years. In addition to Lawrence, his firm served as the auditor for other schools including Berry School located in the same county. Unlike Lawrence, Berry did not participate in the private school division and therefore had a completely different way of approaching and budgeting for financial assistance. Both schools had similar enrollment and both had about the same number of students competing in high school athletics. As Lawrence Academy had been growing, so too was its budget for overall financial assistance. Berry's budget had grown but only modestly by comparison. Here are how the numbers compared: Of Lawrence Academy's $15 million budget, approximately $1.3 million, or about 8 percent, was for financial assistance. Of Berry's $15 million budget, financial assistance was about $600,000, or about 4 percent of the total budget. A significant difference between the two schools.

As was their practice, the Lawrence Academy finance committee of the board met with Jim to discuss the upcoming audit. Not included in that meeting was the Lawrence business manager, John, who had been in that role for more than a decade. Jim and John often clashed, and John was concerned that Jim could not make the distinction between the financial aid budgets at schools like Lawrence and Berry, yet never seemed to have a problem expressing his opinion regardless of knowledge of the subject. The finance committee was relatively ignorant of this difference but clearly had more trust in the auditor than in their business manager. Jim used this opportunity to be highly critical of Lawrence and the excessive amount of financial assistance Lawrence was providing. Jim's "blame" went directly to John, not the head of school. He used the inappropriate example of Berry School to draw his comparison, failing to recognize the differences in the two schools.

The finance committee was captivated by his argument and this further divided the finance committee from the business manager. Later, John attempted to explain to the committee why Jim's position was unfounded. Unfortunately, the committee was no longer listening. They were convinced the expert in this matter was Jim and that John would have to find ways to cut the financial assistance budget. The relationship between the finance committee and business manager was badly damaged and trust between the two was gone. Two years later John resigned. It was years before turnover on the finance committee finally brought better understanding. The school eventually changed auditors.

Questions for Discussion

1. *Why is trust such an important factor between the board and the school's senior leadership?*
2. *What role could the board chair have played?*
3. *What role could the head of school have played?*
4. *What does this story say about board education and committee education on issues unique to independent schools?*

5. *Should the finance committee and the board have "line item veto," or should their approval be primarily the overall budget, trusting the school's leadership to determine the specifics of how resources should be expended?*

Chapter Two

◆

Volunteer Boards—
Volunteer Leaders

Volunteer boards are an essential part of every independent and faith-based school. They are required by state and federal law and therefore play a central role in the school's ability to achieve its mission and vision. When boards are utilized effectively, they can be a major asset and a source of support not found elsewhere. However, if proper leadership and direction are absent, volunteer boards can be a roadblock and actually prevent the school from achieving its goals. At the outset of the process of examining the governing board, there are some of the issues that need to be prioritized:

- Focus on board responsibilities and begin to make a list of what constitutes a dynamic and inspired board. How does the school's mission and vision impact board responsibilities and priorities?
- Analyze the current board in terms of their effectiveness and develop criteria in key areas such as: fundraising, pro-

fessional skills, diversity, advocacy, attendance, participation, etc. Discover what is working well that should be supported and what is not working that should be improved or eliminated.

- Decide what mix of talents make the board most effective. What are the needs that can be addressed by talent and skills represented on the board? Do we really understand the needs, and do we have the capability of attracting these kinds of individuals?

- Consider statements such as the Covenant Agreement or adopt the Governance Promise, documents that provide clear understanding as to the importance of the relationship between the staff and the board. These guiding principles can set expectations and be a road map for current and future board members.

- Develop a manual that includes such information as:

  1. List of current board members, including contact information
  2. Mission statement
  3. Brief history of the school
  4. Marketing and fundraising materials
  5. Meeting calendar for the year
  6. Minutes from the previous year
  7. Other relevant material that would assist a new board member

Board of Trustees vs. Board of Trust: One Board—One Voice

Perhaps it is only a matter of semantics, but it is worth making note of the distinction between a term used widely and to give a little thought to the inferences as well as a term that is used much more sparingly. The board of trustees suggests a group of individuals who act and perform their roles and responsibilities as a group. The board of *trust* suggests that this is a group who act and perform their responsibilities as one cohesive unit. This is not simply semantics but rather a statement about the true meaning of what *trusteeship* encompasses.

Working together with one voice is, or certainly should be, the way in which the best and most effective boards function. Throughout this book reference is made to the board of trustees, but the thought behind this terminology is that these individuals have come together for the greater good and truly function as a board of trust.

CASE STORY #2
Demonstrating Respect for School Leadership

The board of Crawford Academy was not experienced in the search process for a new head of school. The school was about forty years old and had at one time enrolled over a thousand students, but current enrollment was less than eight hundred. None of the current trustees was on the board when the last head was hired. Therefore, it was an easy decision to hire a firm well-known for its work in providing leadership to independent and faith-based schools. There was no question that the board would rely heavily on the expertise of the firm to find candidates that would fit the culture and climate of the school. The firm's representative for the search was Brad, and he made it clear that the process would be lengthy and thorough, but the end result would be the emergence of a great candidate to be the next head of school.

The search firm's representative, Brad, did the necessary preliminary work that included:

- Meeting with constituencies of the school to determine what characteristics would bring the most to the school
- Creating the position description and profile
- Reaching out to key leaders to determine interest level
- Advertising the position in a variety of outlets

As the search process got underway, Brad identified a number of individuals who expressed interest in the position. As in most searches, some candidates appeared to be well-qualified, while others fell far short of the qualities and experience necessary for the position.

One of the most intriguing elements in every head search is whether or not the search will include an internal candidate. In this search, it became clear that the current upper school head, Anna, was very interested in the position. However, she was reluctant to throw her hat in the ring. Anna had been at the school for a number of years and was an alumnus of the school. However, she had heard and observed on several occasions that the board was not functioning at a very high level. The impression among many was that the board was dysfunctional. Eventually Brad convinced her that she would make an excellent candidate and would receive serious consideration for the position. Anna agreed and provided the necessary materials to become a candidate.

In addition to retaining the search firm, the board had created a search committee that included five members of the board. The chair of the board was also the chair of the search committee. Brad had outlined what the committee's responsibilities included and what they did not include. As time went on, there were approximately thirty legitimate applications for the position. Brad narrowed the candidate pool down to ten. The search committee was charged with ranking the ten candidates to determine how many candidates they wanted to conduct initial interviews with, including the possibility of interviewing all ten.

After review, the committee recommended to Brad that they wanted to interview six candidates with the thought of narrowing the six down to three finalists for more extensive interviews to be held at Crawford Academy. When Brad reviewed the six semifinalists, he noticed the head of the upper school was not included. Brad was clearly stunned. Not only did he consider Anna an excellent candidate, he had strongly encouraged her to apply when she had been reluctant to do so. He met with the committee to discuss the six candidates and specifically to learn why they had chosen not to include Anna in the six for further consideration.

The discussion was tense and revealed characteristics Brad found concerning if not alarming. The search committee's rationale for not including Anna among the six semi-finalists made it very clear to Brad that their reasons were not in keeping with the spirit of the process. And, most importantly, they demonstrated almost a complete lack of respect for Anna and her effectiveness in her current leadership role at the school. Given the fact that she held a leadership position, had been in that role for a number of years, was highly respected in the school community, and had credentials (a doctorate)—all experiences other candidates did not have—Brad felt it obvious that an interview would be completely appropriate.

The search committee was not convinced and restated their belief that Anna would not be interviewed. They provided no further explanation. Brad made sure that they understood this would be considered a serious snub, most likely making her feel uncomfortable and unsupported in her current role.

Questions for Discussion

1. *What counsel should a board seek when undertaking the process of beginning a search for a head of school?*
2. *What criteria should be used in selecting the search committee?*
3. *How should the search committee approach the hiring of a search firm?*
4. *There was a strongly held difference of opinion regarding the selection of semi-finalists candidates. What is the best way to resolve this issue?*
5. *Should a strong internal candidate be given the courtesy and respect of an interview?*
6. *What advice would you give Anna going forward?*
7. *What will Brad do differently in the next search he conducts?*

Chapter Three

◆

Trustee Recruitment: Creating a Process for Success

The joint responsibility of the board's committee on trustees or governance committee (the two most-often used names for this committee), all board members, and the school's staff is *recruiting* and *maintaining* the most inspired board members possible. Each of these two components has an important task when considering who to add to the board. The needs of the school must be clear and carefully articulated to a prospective trustee.

The recruitment process is critical. If done in a haphazard manner, the school will not be able to attract the people most needed to serve on the board. Here are some factors to consider:

- *Gender:* It is important to have diversity on the board. Representation on the board should reflect the makeup of the organization's constituency. It is not only the right thing to do; it will also enhance the school in numerous ways.

- *Age:* Having members who represent a range of ages most likely is a healthy way to build the board. All too often boards are made up of older people. While wisdom and experience is significant, a range of ages adds different perspectives and depth.

- *Occupation:* Does the board include expertise and experience in areas that will be helpful? There is value in having different occupations represented; just be sure that you have members with knowledge of finance, marketing, facilities, and other beneficial areas.

- *Ethnicity:* Ethnic diversity adds to the board and to the school in meaningful ways. Having representation from different ethnic groups demonstrates an understanding of the various contributions diverse members bring to the board that can be enormously constructive and beneficial.

- *Recommendation source:* Is the person making the recommendation someone whose opinion is valued and who has the best interest of the school, as opposed to someone who wants to enhance his or her particular agenda?

- *Other board affiliations and interests:* Potential board members have their own spheres of influence—which can be extremely helpful. Be sure you capture this information in the recruitment process. If a prospective board member has served or is currently serving on another board, that information may reveal his or her ability to be an effective and supportive board member.

- *Strengths and specific areas of contribution:* A matrix identifying needs and strengths allows the board to be intentional about what skills and abilities are most needed. For example, if a capital campaign is on the horizon, adding those with knowledge of fundraising, construction, and facilities management might be timely.

- *Representative of the school's constituencies:* Ideally the board should reflect the various constituencies of the school. This could include ethnic diversity, religious background, vocation, demographics, among other factors.

Determine the Compatibility of a Candidate

The process of securing a commitment from a prospective board member is one that requires great care. Here are several examples of ways to determine the compatibility of a prospect with the school and staff:

Invite the Person to Attend an Event

An appropriate priority in recruitment is to find out all you can about a prospective board member. One of the ways to do this is to invite the person to attend an event—either on the school campus or elsewhere. The purpose is to begin to introduce the prospective board member (assuming they are not already completely familiar with the school) to key staff, donors, volunteers, and, of course, other board members. Even if a prospective trustee is a current parent, grandparent, alumnus, former staff member, etc., you should not assume they have the knowledge, skill set, or temperament to be a member of the board.

Seek the Candidate's Assistance or Input on a Committee

Many schools have great success by including non-trustees on board committees. The organization may be seeking the input from someone with specific expertise. The school may recognize the value of someone who may not have the time available to make the commitment to serve on the board. And, the school may ask a non-trustee with the idea of looking at the person as being a potential trustee in the future.

Invite the Candidate to Meet Other Board Members, the Head of School, and the Development and Marketing Staff

Beyond meeting people at an event, it is very important that prospective trustees have opportunities to get to know the school's leadership. This is important for several reasons, but most importantly it helps the candidate become more informed about the school's mission, vision, and programs.

Offer a Tour of the Facilities

Part of the candidate's becoming informed about the school is to see and tour the school's facilities. It demonstrates a commitment by making the effort to physically see the school—it is a component of increasing their knowledge.

Typically, a member of the committee on trustees (perhaps the chair) and the head of school should invite the candidate to meet them. A personal invitation to meet these two individuals should be a strong signal that the school takes the process of adding trustees very seriously. Is this process time-consuming? Yes. Is this process essential to the school's future? Absolutely! Recruiting the best possible trustee will have an enormous impact!

Following the candidate's agreement to serve and approval by the full board, a separate letter of welcome should be sent from the board chair and head of school. The letter should outline arrangements for the board orientation session.

CASE STORY #3
"We Have an Opening on Our Board . . ."

Linda and her husband had recently moved into their townhouse. They loved the location and were thrilled with the independent school they had chosen for their children. Linda enjoyed gardening but especially liked having a confined space to tend her garden— the small yard suited her well. She also really appreciated the fact that one of the responsibilities of the homeowner's association was mowing and landscaping not only the common ground of the complex but also each individual yard. This enabled Linda to focus her outside energy on having the nicest garden possible.

One morning as she was outside working, a neighbor walked by and stopped to talk with her. Linda had never met him, but he was nice and very complimentary of the appearance of the garden and the overall exterior of her home. After a few minutes, they both realized their children attended the same school. As they were discussing the school as well as the topics of plants, trees, gardening, and the importance of such matters, her new neighbor suddenly shifted gears. He unexpectedly announced that, "We have an opening on the school's board of trustees. Would you be interested in being a board member?"

Linda looked at him a long moment and thought to herself, *Is this the most effective way to recruit board members? How serious could this board be when he is asking someone he just met and knows nothing about?* Finally she replied, "Thank you for asking, but that is not something I can do right now. We need to get settled in our new home and learn more about the school." Without missing a beat her new friend responded, "Well, I know there will be another opening in a few months. Perhaps that would be a more convenient time." She noted he said this more as a statement rather than a question. She smiled and decided it best not to react to this. After a few more minutes of idle conversation, he said he had to be going, but that it was nice meeting her.

Questions for Discussion

1. *What is your initial reaction to this encounter?*
2. *What motivated the man to ask Linda to join the board?*
3. *What is your opinion of his approach?*
4. *Do you believe he was authorized to extend that offer?*
5. *What does this episode tell you about the school's board?*
6. *What did Linda's reaction tell you about her?*
7. *What should have happened?*

Chapter Four

◆

Board Member Training and Orientation

In many independent and faith-based schools several board members typically or often join the board at a specified time of the year, thus creating a "class" of new board members. These members begin and potentially are re-elected or rotate off at the same time. This process creates a climate of stability and a level of continuity that will ensure that governance is systematic and follows the guidelines as established in the bylaws.

Orientation

Regardless of the number of new members coming on the board, an orientation session is essential for the reasons described below:

- An orientation session introduces the new board member(s) to officers, key staff members, and other new board members. If they have already met, this will be an opportunity to get to know them better and initiate a relationship that will well serve both the school and the board.

- An orientation session should review the history of the school. There may be new trustees who know the school very well, but never assume anything. Regardless of the level of familiarity, everyone will benefit from a history lesson and likely discover information not previously known.

- An orientation session should describe and review the committee structure of the board. Committee assignments may be made at the orientation session or soon after. With many boards, much of their work is accomplished through committees. Committee review should be an essential part of the orientation session.

- An orientation session should provide the new board member with a manual, or the documentation and materials should be sent electronically. Such a manual should include all pertinent material that the member would need to know in order to be the most effective board member possible.

- An orientation session should set the tone to establish responsibilities and expectations.

- An orientation session will allow the new board member to feel welcome and recognized as a contributing member of the school's board from the beginning. An orientation session dramatically reduces the "learning curve" for new trustees.

- An orientation session should set the tone for the culture of the board. Articulating expectations, discussing appropriate behavior, defining relationships with school staff and faculty, reminding them about such issues of confidentiality, emphasizing service rather power, and placing value on speaking with one voice are critical topics that must be addressed.

Training

There are numerous ways to effectively train or provide ongoing education for members of your board of trustees. Research and best practices collide with the fundamental truth that boards that are better trained and that engage in continuous professional development are significantly more effective in their role. Therefore, they are better positioned to contribute to the board and the school they are serving.

Training can occur in a variety of settings and circumstances. Here are a few to keep in mind:

Board Retreat

The board retreat is a time-tested and proven way in which training as well as evaluation of the board can occur. Topics for retreats can vary but usually fall into a few general categories:

- *Strategic Planning.* Often a board will use a retreat setting to initiate a strategic planning process. Once the process has been completed, the board may use a retreat to conclude the strategic planning process. Both retreats can be highly effective and focused ways in which to address the strategic direction of the school.
- *Board Evaluation.* The board may see a retreat as a way to determine its own effectiveness. Often each trustee completes an evaluation instrument and the results are then shared and discussed during the retreat. Again, a retreat setting can provide focus and purpose by encouraging the board to clearly understand, accept, and carry out their responsibilities. Chapter 17 and Appendix H include an evaluation instrument that may be helpful to your school.

- *Fundraising Campaign.* The decision by a school to consider a major fundraising program usually requires extensive planning. The formulation of that plan, the steps necessary to implement the plan, and deliberations held in a retreat setting may well reveal strengths and concerns regarding the plan.
- *Programmatic Initiatives.* Schools often have a variety of programs and services they provide as a part of their mission and vision. The board retreat can be a venue for dialogue as to whether additions, deletions, or changes to programs should be considered. The genesis of fundraising campaigns and programmatic reviews may well be the strategic planning process.
- *General Business of the School.* Board retreats may also be similar to a regular meeting in terms of the agenda but may take place in a setting that allows the board to bond and build stronger relationships over a more extended period of time beyond what a regular meeting would allow.

The experience of a board retreat is often enhanced by the presence and guidance of an experienced facilitator or consultant. This individual should be brought in as an independent resource capable of providing experience, perspective, wisdom, and respect to the entire proceeding. Having such a person lead the process tends to allow everyone—board, head of school, staff—more freedom to actively participate in the discussion. Every school should conduct retreats and should budget for a consultant to help achieve the results needed for success. It is this type of investment that separates schools that thrive from those that merely survive.

Seminar or Workshop

Many independent and faith-based professional associations at the national, regional, state, and even local level offer all manner of workshop and seminar opportunities for trustees. There is an enormous emphasis placed on these opportunities because of the recognition that governance is so significant to the school and that board development is linked directly to achieving potential.

A critical aspect of seminars and workshops is the opportunity for both the board chair and head of school to participate together. There is little that is more valuable than for the chair and the head to hear, discuss, and question the same message concerning the impact of these two leaders on the school's future.

While more such opportunities would be helpful, the real challenge is for the board chair and members of the board to discover the important impact of these sessions.

We will always have a need for more professional associations to provide more opportunities to discuss board development issues and for there to be more opportunities for heads and board chairs to attend together on issues of mutual interest and benefit to the school.

Leadership Coaching

Often overlooked and not completely understood is the opportunity for boards, board chairs, and heads to participate in leadership coaching. This "personal trainer" concept can be enormously beneficial to the individuals involved and can lead to better self-awareness, stronger relationships, and school enhancements.

Inspired boards are ones that work well together. Board education through retreats, seminars, workshops, and coaching is an enormously important investment the school can make in its future.

CASE STORY #4
Shifting Expectations

The interview had gone well. Robert was not very surprised. He'd had many phone conversations and e-mail communications with the chair of the search committee. It was obvious and gratifying that Robert and Carl had already established a very positive relationship. Robert was excited about the prospect of becoming the head of school at this well-known if fairly new independent school. If it all worked out, this would be his third, and probably last, school where he would serve as the head. Robert would turn fifty-three in the fall.

Carl and the entire search committee had been very positive. Robert was anxious to hear as much as possible about the working relationship between the head of school and board. He asked every question he could think of and wanted to be as certain as possible regarding expectations and how his performance would be evaluated. Carl seemed to be very positive and receptive to Robert's inquiries.

A few weeks later Robert was offered the position. He and Carl discussed major points to put into a letter of agreement and ultimately a contract. Robert should have seen some problems brewing when the draft of his contract was over twenty pages! Alarms did go off, but he was not overly concerned with the length or the language in the document.

At the end of the first year everything changed. For personal reasons Carl had to leave the board, and the transition to the new chair had been awkward. Don had been a member of the board, but in the last twelve months, he had been elevated to vice chair and treasurer. His priorities and expectations for Robert were very different than those of Carl. And suddenly, Don was the new chair!

Mostly unknown to Robert when he arrived at the school, there was a significant financial commitment with a schedule that called for a million-dollar payment eighteen months after he began as head of school. Robert had been told that the payment was being renegotiated and that if Robert could reduce the amount by half that would signal the bankers of the efforts the school was making. He was determined to reduce this by more if possible.

During the eighteen-month period with Robert's leadership and experience as a fundraiser, he had managed to lead efforts that resulted in over eight hundred thousand dollars given toward the million-dollar goal. Robert had assumed that the board would view this as a very positive move in ultimately reaching the goal. But he failed to recognize Don's insistence that all of the money be committed. With no notice, the board's expectations of Robert had been shifted. With no warning he would be evaluated on a goal that was completely unrealistic.

Questions for Discussion

1. *What red flags can you see regarding Robert's contract?*
2. *Why are transitions between two board chairs so often difficult?*
3. *What conclusions can you draw regarding what Robert was told by Carl and others on the finance committee?*
4. *What is your opinion regarding what to share with a prospective candidate?*

Chapter Five

◆

Establishing the Vital Role of the Committee on Trustees

The independent and faith-based school board of trustees is critical to the effective operation of the school—not because the board has day-to-day oversight but rather because of their fiduciary, mission, vision, strategic direction responsibilities, and their role in hiring and supporting the head of school. Board members come to their roles as trustees from a variety of perspectives, backgrounds, and constituencies. Therefore, they require training and education as to what constitutes being a valuable and valued trustee.

Tradition suggests that many independent and faith-based schools had a nominating committee whose principle responsibility was identifying prospective trustees, contacting them (usually by phone) just prior to the board meeting, and presenting the slate of candidates to the full board for consideration (sometimes the next day). In this process, there was often little thought given to actual needs or skills or any understanding of the work or culture of the board nor any explanation of expectations. All too often this looked a lot like the "good ol' boy network" in which the nominating committee was reaching out primarily to friends, not thinking too seriously about diversity, other issues, or considerations in regards to what and how that could benefit the school. This should not suggest that all nominating committees have such a narrow view of their roles. Certainly, there are boards with nominating committees who view their role broadly, taking into consideration a range of responsibilities that incorporate many of the issues a committee on trustees would consider essential. However, the terminology used by many schools is to establish as a standing committee a committee on trustees, or as it is sometimes referred to, the governance committee.

The committee on trustees truly must have a broad range of responsibilities that goes beyond what the traditional nominating committee was asked to consider. Therefore, this committee is typically assigned with the following responsibilities:

Responsibility 1: Identifying Prospective Trustees

One of the most important roles for the board of trustees is to develop an ongoing list of prospective trustees—individuals who can bring the skills needed to provide the support and expertise to advance the school. This list should be compiled with input from a range of sources and reviewed in anticipation of recruiting the next group or class of trustees. The committee on trustees should meet well in advance of any deadline to ensure that a thorough review can take place to prioritize board candidates.

Responsibility 2: Developing the Recruiting Process and Plan

The process of recruiting trustees must be strategic and intentional. A genuine action plan that has the steps necessary to engage those most suited to contribute is required. Such a plan should include:

- When and with whom the initial contact is made
- Setting up a meeting to discuss being on the board
- Determining who is most compatible with the prospective trustee
- Selecting an appropriate setting for the visit to occur
- Following up and establishing the next action steps
- Creating a welcome strategy

These steps may seem to be too much, perhaps more than potentially necessary. Each school has to set the right tone, attitude, and methodology to ensure the process is yielding the most candidates desirable. Every school will approach this task in a way that reflects their organizational culture. Nevertheless, every school must understand that these elements, however they are carried out, must be included when recruiting trustees.

Responsibility 3: Meeting with Each Prospective Trustee

This is a mandatory and critical step in trustee recruiting. All too often the board nominating committee, as some are referred to, believes it is unnecessary to actually hold a face-to-face meeting with a prospective trustee. There are four questions the board must ask itself before embarking on this strategic mistake:

1. Do they believe that anyone and everyone is clamoring to be on their board?

2. Are they unaware that competition for volunteer board members is actually intense?
3. Have they been lazy and simply waited until the last minute to discover that it's now too late?
4. Have they not been trained or in some way guided to understand how dangerous this is?

The elements of this meeting in terms of *when, where, who,* and *what* will determine how valuable it will ultimately be. *When,* of course, has to do with the timing of when new trustees begin their service—typically found in the bylaws. *Where* the meeting takes place should be casual and friendly while at the same time setting a serious tone—a breakfast or lunch is usually an excellent venue. *Who* should meet with the new trustee? It depends, but the chair of the committee on trustees as well as the head of school should be there, and perhaps the chair of the board. Possibly someone on the board who is close to the prospective trustee may also be included. *What* is conveyed is the final piece of the puzzle, but the conversation must include:

1. Information about the school (included in packet)
2. List of trustees (included in packet)
3. Promotional materials (included in packet)
4. A time for questions and answers specifically designed to determine the attitude and perspective of the person being recruited
5. Stories and "case studies" designed to reveal expectations and best practices
6. Specific discussion of fundraising and its importance to the school along with the role of each trustee
7. Discussion of board culture that clearly shows the board's stance on conflicts of interest, confidentiality, hidden agendas, and any other relevant issues

Responsibility 4: Developing an Orientation Session for New Trustees.

If the committee on trustees has done their job in recruiting the best trustees, then the orientation session has every possibility of being successful. If they have not been able to attract excellent trustees, but only those trustees who come with an agenda or trustees who possess a poor attitude toward their role, then an orientation session will have limited impact.

The orientation session ideally reinforces what the new trustee heard when being recruited. It should address a range of issues including:

- Role of head of school
- Relationship between head of school and board
- Meeting schedule
- Committee structure
- Bylaws
- Minutes
- Expectations

Responsibility 5: Providing Continuing Education of Trustees Through Retreats and Other Professional Development Opportunities.

Professional development opportunities for trustees is one area of board development that frequently lacks attention. Conferences, workshops, and seminars devoted to topics and issues that support trustees will help them to thrive in their job. It is critical that trustees be engaged in these types of activities and seek out opportunities to improve and be better board members.

Many boards conduct retreats and frequently on an annual basis. Retreats come in a variety of shapes and formats—meaning there is no single model that works best. Here are some effective ways to conduct a retreat:

- Hold a retreat annually.
- If possible, meet in a location away from the school's campus.
- Meet in a location that is as free from distractions and disruptions as possible.
- Build into the agenda time specifically to work on team-building, including opportunities for fellowship and socializing.
- Focus discussion on long-range visioning (strategic planning) issues, fundraising/advancement/marketing issues, major programmatic initiatives, facility priorities, or financial matters.
- Stay away from day-to-day issues.
- Set aside time to conduct a board meeting and possibly committee meetings.
- Leave the retreat with an action plan and assignments that resulted from the retreat.

Responsibility 6: Developing the Process of Evaluation for Each Trustee and the Entire Board.

The process by which the board is tasked with considering their own effectiveness is, for some schools, a challenge. There is a level of uncertainty as to what this looks like and how the results will be utilized. The argument is sometimes made that the board is made up of volunteers who simply do not have the time to add this additional time commitment to their plates. Of course, the counterargument is that to do the best job possible for an institution that is providing an excellent educational experience for students and to be ahead of the curve when it comes to best practices, the board should be engaged in some type of evaluation.

While results are important, the magic is in the process—participating in evaluation and reflection with the intent of getting better is a win for the board and a win for the school. The evaluation instrument found in this book (Appendix H) is one way to measure effectiveness. There are others. The key is to believe that evaluation is important and to develop a mechanism for the evaluation to happen. The board chair must take the lead to ensure this is a priority for the board.

Responsibility 7: Partnering with the Head of School Regarding Trustee Recruitment and Education.

Although not universally true, in most of the independent and faith-based schools the head is considered to be the only employee of the board of trustees. The success of this reporting relationship is the key to school effectiveness. It is the foundation on which the school thrives. In its absence the viability of the school is significantly diminished.

The capacity to move the school from this relationship to a true partnership between the head and the trustees demonstrates an understanding of how this can transform the school. At the heart of this partnership is the realization that the head of school and board chair must collaborate and establish a model as a way of working together. There may be nothing more important than this single issue!

Final Thought

Often overlooked or not proactively considered is the idea of recruiting trustees who demonstrate a positive attitude—individuals who consistently show that they are optimistic and who look for the best in individuals and circumstances. Of course, this does not altogether replace skills, experience, or expertise. But knowledge and wisdom are not the same. It is likely that people with these characteristics will help provide a perspective that is all too often lost on a culture seeking the worst and finding fault when such an attitude is not healthy or productive.

The committee on trustees truly has a significant impact on the board's ability to do their job with a sense of effectiveness and accomplishment. When considering what makes a difference in a best-practices board versus one that is dysfunctional, the committee on trustees tops the list of the group charged with having the most influence.

CASE STORY #5
When Discussion Is Mandatory

Sam stared at the e-mail and was somewhat stunned by what he was seeing. He certainly knew that there were decisions that could be made by e-mail, but a decision like this seemed to him to require a genuine discussion and not merely a response to a vote by e-mail.

The e-mail was about a trustee, Ted, who was proposing to build and completely fund a new indoor football practice complex at the independent school where Sam served as a trustee. Such a facility would be wonderful to have. However, this was not a priority and not something in the strategic plan. Ted seemed not to have any concern for what was included in the strategic plan but rather his concern ended with what he believed to be most needed for the school.

Ted's offer seemed too good to be true. He volunteered to construct the facility and completely pay for it—regardless of cost. But there was a catch—the school would have no opportunity to determine the appearance of the facility. Ted was a contractor and knew best about how to fit it in to the rest of the campus. To Sam this appeared problematic. The board would have no oversight into any aspect of this construction project estimated at about $2 million.

The e-mail, sent from the chair of the board, was asking for the board to vote on whether or not to move forward on this construction project. It was clear that the executive committee and building and grounds committee had already voted in favor of the project. In the end Sam went along with his trustee colleagues and voted in favor of the project.

Two years later the building was complete. While it was not compatible with other campus buildings, it could have been worse. Because this project became the priority, capital projects in the strategic plan were put on hold. Although Ted had repeatedly promised that the building would not cost the school any money, cost overruns were over $100,000, and Ted was very slow to complete his commitment. In fact, the auditors were raising questions as to whether or not the school should write off as a loss the money he still owed toward completing the project.

Questions for Discussion

1. *What is your opinion about voting by e-mail?*
2. *How should the chair and the executive committee address trustees who have agendas?*
3. *Why do you believe Sam voted with the other trustees?*
4. *Although this project was not part of the strategic direction, should it have been considered?*
5. *How do you believe the school should have responded when it became obvious Ted had little intention of paying what was owed?*
6. *Should the bylaws be consulted regarding how a vote is taken?*
7. *Do you believe someone like Ted would have benefitted from participating in a trustee workshop?*

Chapter Six

♦

Determining Responsibilities and Priorities of the Board

As the governing body for the independent and faith-based school, the board of trustees has numerous responsibilities, some of which are mandated by the organization's articles of incorporation and bylaws. As with most topics and issues addressed in this book, there are numerous lists and definitions as to a board's role and responsibilities. The list that follows is one way in which to determine board responsibilities and priorities:

1. Set Forth the School's Mission

This responsibility is perhaps the most discussed and the best known. The mission (statement) is the school's reason for being and the strategic articulation of who it is and who it wants to become. This is the collective responsibility of all board members and should be well understood by each member.

2. Work Together and Intentionally to Ensure Success for the Head of School

This may be the least understood responsibility of the board. All too often referred to as the "hire and fire" statement, what the board should strive for is an authentic spirit of partnership, collaboration, understanding, and support. To suggest "hiring and firing" is the way to describe this responsibility is one dimensional and misses a genuine opportunity to communicate what working together is truly all about. This does not preclude the reporting nature of the head and the fact that the board has only one employee. The significance of expressing the relationship in this way makes clear what is really at stake—working together is central to this relationship, and this is a responsibility of the entire board.

3. Ensure that Vigorous Strategic Planning is a Priority

All planning should be strategic! The considered and deliberate way to move forward is a significant priority of the board. This takes on different formats for different organizations. The intent, however, must remain constant—to review where you have been, determine where you want to go, and create the steps needed to make that change. Often the strategic planning committee oversees this process as a part of their direct responsibilities. All committees and all board members have a stake to ensure the process is active, meaningful, and inclusive.

4. Ensure Adequate Financial Resources Are in Place

Financial solvency and sustainability are obviously keys to the school's viability. Nonprofit does not mean "no money"! From the perspective of the board, the treasurer and the finance committee have the specific charge for ensuring the budget is balanced and that the financial records are in order—and confirmed by an independent auditing process. However, the fiduciary responsibility is every trustee's responsibility. Some trustees and heads believe that every board member at one time during their tenure should sit in on meetings of the finance committee to get a better understanding of the issues faced by the school. Not a bad idea.

We speak today of transparency and must understand that not only is it the right thing to do but helps assure the constituency that the school has nothing to hide and is operating according to appropriate accounting guidelines and practices. This does not imply that you post your budget on your web site or that you allow anyone and everyone to look at whatever their particular issue or concern might be. What it does mean is that you listen to such a request and determine whether or not it would address a legitimate concern.

On occasion a parent of the school might ask to see the budget. Upon further inquiry and listening, the head can often determine the nature of the request and can discuss the issue without revealing specific numbers.

5. Make Giving to the School a Priority

This is one of those issues that never fails to surface and is almost always controversial. If someone is a member of the board of trustees then giving to the school should be a philanthropic priority—at least during the time the person is serving as a trustee. Period! No exceptions. Two things are at issue here. First, it is the responsibility of the committee on trustees to make it crystal clear what the expectations are with respect to trustee giving. This must be done before someone is asked to join the board, *not* after. Second, make certain that board members know they are not required to contribute the same amount, but rather to be as generous as possible given each individual's circumstances. This is often referred to as equal sacrifice, not equal giving.

6. Manage All Resources Effectively

All resources encompass everything including endowment performance, physical plant, budget, audit, and the operation of the business office. It is expected that there are board members who have the knowledge and expertise to understand endowment performance, managing of the facilities, including depreciation of assets, and the other issues critical to a successful, sustainable operation. Again, the committee on trustees must recognize this need and find the right people who can provide wisdom in these often complex areas. While the school's business manager reports to the head, this person works closely with the board treasurer and chair of the finance committee—often this is the same individual. The business manager must possess the experience and financial expertise to converse knowledgeably with the treasurer. Nowhere is trust, collaboration, and respect needed more than in the working relationship between these two.

7. Do Not Engage in Conflicts of Interest

Often discussed but seldom understood is the definition of "conflict of interest." Such behavior is unacceptable, unethical, and erodes trust among everyone familiar with the school. Any potential conflict of interest must be declared. Simply stated, a conflict of interest exists when a board member joins the board with the purpose of seeking to gain an advantage as a board member by securing business or favors that are unfairly or inappropriately obtained. It is a complex and frequently misunderstood occurrence. Two examples seem appropriate.

The first involves a board member who is also a contractor. The school is renovating a building and this contractor is one of the bidders for this job. The school reviews several bids—including the one from the board member. Is this a conflict of interest? No. The board member was not seeking to receive special treatment or an unfair advantage by virtue of serving on the board.

The second example involves a board member who is also a stockbroker. This individual joins the board and hopes that by doing so he can align himself to solicit other trustees to become his clients. Is this a conflict of interest? Yes. This trustee is using his position to influence others on the board to do business. Further, if the broker trustee does in fact do business with other trustees, and to potentially keep a client happy, he or she supports that client's positions to maintain that business relationship. That is an enormous conflict of interest and has the potential to cause damage to the school.

8. In Conjunction With the Head of School, Monitor the School's Programs and Services

It is not the board's responsibility to manage the day-to-day operation of the school. Trustees, however, are responsible to be attentive to the programs, services, marketing, new initiatives, etc. These are areas in which the trustees' relationship with the head becomes an advantage. Being well-informed with programs and services will make for a better and valued trustee.

9. Enhance the School's Public Image

While not often considered a responsibility of the board, the public perception of the school is in fact the responsibility of everyone closely connected—which includes the board of trustees. It may be both appropriate and helpful to have on the board individuals with expertise and experience in the areas of marketing, branding, communications, and public relations. Trustees are both advocates and ambassadors for the school. They should be equipped with information that will allow them to speak with confidence.

10. Embrace the Concept of Confidentiality

It is not enough to talk the talk—you have to walk the walk. In other words, this concept must be clearly articulated as an expectation. Schools and their boards of trustees are not immune to rumors and gossip, social media attacks, or other forms of improper communication. Most of us understand the TV ad campaign that states, "What happens in Vegas, stays in Vegas!" The work of the board and the discussions and decisions that result are not to be shared in a publicly. To be sure, certain public organizations are subject to laws that determine what must be public record. That is not the issue here.

How do you reconcile transparency while at the same time keeping confidential certain information? As a 501(c)(3) school, you are well within both your rights and responsibilities to not share certain information. The board of trustees has the legal and fiduciary responsibility to manage and direct the school as they see fit—according to the language of the charter and bylaws.

There are some schools in which the board chair begins every meeting reminding the board about the importance of confidentiality. Verbal reminders may be helpful, but it is the actions of the board that determine whether or not adherence to this principle is taken seriously.

11. Evaluate the Board's Performance

All too often boards don't adequately evaluate their own performance or effectiveness. In fact, many boards do not do this at all. When they do it, is it anecdotal with little data of value or impact? There are numerous ways in which evaluation can be accomplished, but none of it matters if the board chair and the officers of the board place little or no value in the process.

It is more than a little ironic that the same board that refuses to evaluate how well they do what they are supposed to be doing is the same group who will place significance on evaluating the head of school. In spite of what some boards think, it works both ways! And because it works both ways, the school is the beneficiary of this way of conducting business. The board must evaluate what they do and how they perform.

* * *

Above all, the board's responsibility has everything to do with the viability of the school—ensuring the long-term sustainability of the school. In certain schools and circumstances the board may believe they need to be more involved in the school's operation. However, the board should still recognize the fact that their role differs greatly from that of the staff. The evidence is overwhelming that best practicing boards are the ones who have an effective process for hiring and working with the head and allowing the head to manage the daily affairs of the school.

CASE STORY #6
Governing by Intimidation

Board bullying may be defined as a situation in which a board member attempts to threaten and intimidate the school's leader or someone on his or her staff. The board member is using his or her position of authority to belittle and place the head of school in an awkward position.

Walt and Phil did not look forward to visiting Carl at his office. The purpose of the visit was to solicit Carl for his gift to the campaign. Actually, the purpose of the visit was to follow up on a gift solicitation made earlier by Walt and another member of the board. Walt, the school's head, and Phil, the vice president for development, had been calling on Carl, a member of the board for the past three years. To Walt and Phil, Carl represented everything that gave a bad name to trustees. He was arrogant, deceitful, talked much more than he listened, and never admitted he was wrong about any issue.

The conversation opened with numerous pleasantries and an assurance of a gift—including, however, much criticism of the wording on the gift commitment card. Soon the conversation turned to the recent board election. Walt and Phil expressed genuine excitement about the new members' potential and looked forward to working with them. Carl's response to their excitement was both unexpected and totally inappropriate. He remarked, "The new members will be supportive (of Walt and Phil) for a year, but if you do not produce in terms of successful fundraising, they will turn on you." Carl's arrogance and willingness to speak on behalf of the new board members without having any idea of what he was saying seemed both ridiculous and intimidating. Was this a threat? Was this a warning? Did the board member have inside information about the new board members that would lead him to make this statement? Or was he merely stating his own bias as to how he felt about the school's leader? Walt knew it would do little good to argue or respond. He did ask Carl, "Do you believe that there is something that we are not doing but should be doing?" There was no response to his question.

This story stands out because it reflects and reveals the complete lack of sensitivity and understanding that Carl has for his role. This type of bullying is one in which someone uses their position in an improper way. Whether intended or not, the statement by the board member was threatening to the head. This was in every way unacceptable behavior. As a private conversation it would be difficult for such a conversation to make its way to the board chair. But it should have. Walt should have gone to the chair—not as someone telling on someone or whining about any mistreatment, but rather to expose unacceptable behavior from someone who is supposed to be a partner and supporter. And the board chair should have confronted Carl about what kind of communication is appropriate behavior. Certainly, conflict of this kind is unpleasant, but there is no alternative to facing it.

The most effective board members are those who partner with the leadership of the school. Working together to achieve common goals, board members and staff leaders are responsible for the stability and future of the school. Intimidation is best avoided by a committee on trustees that do their job and select the best possible trustees.

Questions for Discussion

1. *Do you know trustees like Carl?*
2. *Would you have reacted in the same way as Walt and Phil?*
3. *Why do you believe Carl treats people this way?*
4. *If you were the board chair, describe how you have handled this situation?*
5. *What can the recruitment process do to prevent this from happening?*

Chapter Seven

♦

Creating the Template for Effective Strategic Planning

It is well-documented that the board of trustees of independent and faith-based schools have numerous responsibilities. The fundamental ones are creating the mission statement, hiring and supporting the head of school, overseeing fiduciary and financial matters, and strategic planning.

A Successful Strategic Planning Path

Strategic planning has everything to do with ensuring that the school has a viable, sustainable future, and that the board and administration have reviewed all factors in developing a plan that recognizes the unique characteristics of their school. A number of essential steps, when addressed and followed properly, will provide the most benefit to the school. While there are many avenues to a well-done strategic planning process, the following outline has proven to be a successful path.

Step One: Begin the strategic planning process with a board retreat.

The strategic planning process is a process designed to establish vision, direction, purpose, and should include specific priorities and time frames for focusing on issues determined to be of the greatest significance in the ensuing three- to five-year period. A board retreat is considered to be the most valuable method to begin the strategic planning process. Such a retreat might typically be away from campus and free from day-to-day distractions and it can be held over a one- or two-day time period. While schools will fluctuate on who attends the retreat, it is typical to include all current trustees and the senior administrative leadership of the school. It might also include senior faculty members.

Step Two: Review the school's mission statement.

Almost every independent and faith-based school has a mission statement in which the unique characteristics and aspirations of the school are succinctly articulated to convey vision and purpose. The length and breadth of these mission statements vary from a few words to more than a paragraph. Each board must determine what works best for its circumstances.

The concept or belief behind the wording of the mission statement should remain constant as possible. Changes should primarily be considered when the board is embarking on a new or updated strategic planning process. Often the decision is made to stay with current wording even if the strategic planning process includes consideration of significant changes to certain aspects of the school. This may be the case because the mission statement can incorporate changes while still maintaining the integrity of the intent of the statement. There is also the possibility that as the process unfolds, the current mission statement may not accurately reflect the changes that are approved by the board. At that point, changes to the mission statement should be considered.

Step Three: Engage an outside facilitator to conduct the retreat.

There are at least two very practical reasons why this step is necessary. First, the board needs to have someone outside the board and staff to serve in this role thus allowing all trustees and staff to be completely engaged in the discussion of issues that impact the future of the school. Second, a facilitator will usually have the experience and expertise in working with schools on the strategic planning process. Perhaps this person is a former head of school or trustee as well as someone who has been through the process on several occasions and has dealt with the types of issues and conversations that are likely to surface during the retreat. He or she can also keep the retreat on track by limiting sidebar conversations that might distract or actually hijack the direction of the process.

Step Four: Engage in a thorough brainstorming session, including a SWOT (Strengths, Weaknesses, Opportunities, Threats) Analysis.

From the outset of the retreat the focus should be on creating or expanding on a vision of what is possible. The question that should be addressed by the board of trustees and those participating in the retreat is, What would we like for our school to look like in five years (or some other time period) and what are the steps necessary to achieve that goal?

The timetable is noteworthy. Articulating a vision without a timeframe is not based in reality. This discussion should be wide open with everyone given the opportunity to share thoughts, ideas, and direction for the school. The attitude most needed is the one in which all ideas about the school's future are considered. This is the step in the process when ideas are eliminated as being to far-reaching, costly, or simply deemed unrealistic. That will become apparent as the process moves forward.

Step Five: Organize information into sections and allow for different priorities of the school to be examined both individually and as part of the bigger-picture vision of the school.

The thorough brainstorming session and issues analysis should reveal a far-reaching list of issues, challenges, ideas, and direction that must be turned into priorities and components, on which the school board will focus its attention over the next several months and years. This is the launch pad for what is to follow in the process of putting together a strategic plan for the school.

Step Six: Once all ideas have been brought forward, group the ideas into identifiable sections or categories that correspond to different aspects of the school.

This is the beginning of a more formal process as the board of trustees takes all of the different ideas and places them within existing components or possibly creates new components where something had not existed before. Here are some examples of categories to place ideas acknowledged in the brainstorming process:

- Curriculum or academic program
- Athletics
- Marketing and communications
- Enrollment management
- Financial

- Development
- Capital needs
- Staffing
- Facilities and physical plant

Of course, there could be others, and there could be an initiative that does not adequately fall into an existing category.

Step Seven: Determine the precise role of the board of trustees.

While it is true that strategic planning is a fundamental responsibility of the board of trustees of an independent or faith-based school, the manner in which this is carried out varies from one school to another. Some boards are very hands-on preferring to be directly involved in every aspect of the plan. Other schools believe that the strategic plan should be developed primarily by consultants—individuals who the board believes has substantial experience and expertise in strategic planning for independent schools.

Both approaches have merit, and both approaches can produce the kind of plan the school finds valuable. However, the board manages the process. In the end, it is the board and only the board that votes for the adoption of the plan. And ultimately it is the board's responsibility to see that the plan is implemented on the timetable that has been approved.

Step Eight: Establish the strategic planning committee and outline its responsibilities.

Each school must determine how best to organize and implement the plan the board has approved. For sound, organizational practice as well as a proven method for implementing the strategic plan, many boards have created a strategic planning committee. Whether an ongoing, standing committee of the board (as identified and described in the bylaws) or an ad hoc committee created for this single purpose, the strategic planning committee is created with the two objectives:

1. Ensure that the process is thorough, inclusive, and results in a plan that is meaningful.
2. Establish a process that results in implementing the plan's various components.

Unless dictated by what is in the bylaws, the board has logistical leeway as to how the committee should be established. One possible scenario calls for the executive committee or committee on trustees to consider possible candidates from the board to serve in this role.

Regardless of how the board moves forward in the planning process, the chair of the strategic planning committee should be a current member of the school's board of trustees. The remainder of the strategic planning committee may come from the sub-committee chairs who have identified areas on which to place special emphasis or priority. Both board and non-board members may be invited to be a part of the strategic planning committee.

Step Nine: Seek input from stakeholders by gathering information regarding the school's future.

In order for it to be a legitimate, comprehensive plan, many schools collect information from stakeholders—those individuals who have a connection to the school and, therefore, have reasons why they wish to help shape the future of the school. These stakeholders might include:

- Faculty and staff
- Parents
- Parents of alumni
- Alumni
- Grandparents
- Former trustees
- Special friends of the school
- Community leaders

Typically, the methodology for gathering this information is through a survey or a series of surveys that includes questions designed to provide the kind of information determined to be useful to address the issues on which the school is seeking information—the areas identified as priorities.

Step Ten: Conduct focus group session(s) to obtain more detailed or specific information.

While surveys are valuable and provide the school with information beneficial to the process, a focus group can elicit information not obtained in any other manner. Focus groups may involve a single constituency (parents) or may include multiple constituencies (parents, alumni, grandparents). The facilitator conducting the focus group session should have a series of prepared questions to learn more about certain issues. In addition, the facilitator should sense the attitude, issues, and concerns of the focus group and be prepared to follow the course of a particular discussion to see where it might lead. This flexibility may well provide insight beyond what could have been anticipated by following only a predetermined format. Additionally, simply by being asked to participate as part of the inner circle, members of the focus group are usually motivated to contribute to the strategic planning process.

Step Eleven: Launch the strategic planning committee and sub-committee.

Once various sections have been established and prioritized and after you have gathered additional information through surveys and focus groups, the strategic planning committee is ready to do its work. For example, if the school has decided that there are five sections on which to focus their attention, then it follows that there five different sub-committees, each with their own chair. That sub-committee chair then becomes a part of the strategic planning committee. The sub-committees can include other trustees, administrative staff, faculty members, or others in the community. Best practice suggests that sub-committee chairs should be members of the board.

Over the ensuing several months the sub-committees meet and hammer out the goal for their committee and the various strategies needed to complete the goals in their specific areas.

The strategic planning committee (chair plus all sub-committee chairs) should meet periodically to ensure coordination of sections, address any overlap or conflicts that might arise, and ensure that the sections are not acting as silos but rather as a cohesive unit that understands that all components work together for the betterment of the entire school.

Step Twelve: Once the strategic planning committee has completed a draft of the plan, it must be presented to the full board for a vote.

Part of the board's "ownership" of the plan is a formal vote to adopt the plan—with or without any additional modification. This is best achieved in another retreat-type setting in which the only focus is on the plan. Each sub-committee chair makes their presentation, the chair of the strategic planning committee wraps up the process in a way that gives the full board confidence in the process, and the board then makes a decision to adopt the plan and establish the process by which the plan will be implemented.

Step Thirteen: Begin the process of implementing the plan to ensure that it is continually being addressed and completed in a manner consistent with what the plan calls for.

Strategic plans more often than not fail because they lack the process for a board of trustees to actually implement what the plan calls for. There are several ways to avoid this, but the one often considered effective is one in which strategic planning progress is an agenda item at all board meetings following the adoption of the plan. In this way, the plan will remain at the forefront of everyone's mind since it will be discussed at every board meeting. The chair of strategic planning committee should be called upon for a report and he or she can call on one or more of the sub-committee chairs to come forward with updates of their specific section of the report.

Step Fourteen: Produce a document that provides a summary of the plan that can be shared with all of the School's constituencies.

Confidence from the independent or faith-based school's constituency can be gained by providing a level of transparency when it comes to communicating the context of the plan. Design an attractive document that touches on the highlights of the plan and provides a summary of what is included in the plan. The school may decide what other means (e.g. website, newsletter, magazine, etc.) by which it can appropriately and successfully spread the word about the plan and the school's plans for its implementation.

* * *

While the strategic plan is a vital document that outlines future vision and priorities for the school, the key to its success is recognizing that it is not the document that is essential but rather the process that has been put in place to ensure that over the specified time pertinent issues have been identified and proper plans have been implemented, thus ensuring the brightest possible future for the school.

The fourteen steps described in this chapter provide but a brief overview of the various ways a strategic plan can establish a road map that leads to success. Getting somewhere as opposed to anywhere cannot adequately be accomplished without a proper road map to guide the way.

CASE STORY #7
The Board's Role in Student Discipline

They thought they were very clever and were certain that they had gotten away with it. Three students, all juniors at Donovan Christian Academy, had embarked on a mission to place cameras inside the girls' locker room. Their plan had been to place the cameras in the ceiling and use the ceiling tiles to hinder anyone noticing the cameras. Although "integrity" and "character" were included in the school motto, apparently that was not a priority for these students. Only a few days into this cruel and demeaning episode their world came crashing down. The cameras were discovered!

Following a brief investigation, the identity of the students was proven and they confessed to what they had done. Richard, head of school and Gary, the upper school principal, made the decision that the students would be expelled without the possibility for readmission. It was obvious to the school's leadership that such an offense came with the severest consequence. While there were undoubtedly situations where grace and second chances enter into the decision, Richard and Gary both knew that their responsibility was to make the decision that was in the best interest of Donovan Christian Academy. For them, expulsion was the only way to move forward.

Unfortunately, the parents of the guilty students took exception to the decision and met with the head of school to make their case. The head of school agreed to meet and after a somewhat heated exchange he reminded the parents of the sexual assault nature of what the students had done. He told them that he would not be changing the original judgement resulting in expulsion. The parents then asked if there was any way in which the decision could be appealed. Richard shrugged and made the strategic mistake of indicating that they could appeal the decision to the board.

The parents seized on this opportunity and went to the chair of the Donovan board and requested that the board reconsider the expulsion decision. They met with Justin, the board chair, to make their case. Justin, knowing that the decision had already been made by Richard and Gary to expel the students, told the parents that he would take their appeal to the board's executive committee. By this time the students had been suspended for about two weeks. A few days later the executive committee met to discuss the case. During their discussion, they never spoke with Richard or Gary regarding why they made the decision to expel the students. What they did discuss was that the students were really fine young men who had made a very poor decision. Was expulsion really necessary? Wouldn't suspension have the same effect, or send the same message? At least two of the members of the executive committee knew these students well and another had taught one of the students in his Sunday school class.

In the end, the executive committee overturned the decision of both Richard and Gary. This was never brought to the full board and, therefore, they never had an opportunity to vote on the matter. Justin communicated the ruling to the parents who were understandably elated. It was no surprise that Richard felt he had been betrayed and his authority questioned. Although in some respects he made his peace with the board, he never fully recovered from this incident and a year later resigned as head of school.

This incident was a strategic disaster for the board as they lost their way in terms of what is and what is not their responsibility. For years afterward the board's operational meddling was the cause of significant instability in the school. This resulted in declining enrollment and a genuine loss of reputation in the community.

Questions for Discussion

1. *What did the student handbook say regarding appealing disciplinary decisions made by the administration?*
2. *How should Richard have responded when asked about appealing the expulsion decision?*
3. *Knowing of the school's decision, what should Justin's response have been when asked by the parents to overturn the expulsion decision?*
4. *Why was this appeal never heard by the full board?*
5. *What does best practices tell us about this issue?*
6. *Why does the board's involvement in such issues occur frequently?*
7. *Why do schools struggle with handling disciplinary issues?*
8. *What can be learned from this story and how can Donovan Christian Academy, or any school, move forward with clarity and purpose?*

Chapter Eight

◆

The Five Most Important Responsibilities of the Board Chair

The WAG MORE, BARK LESS, bumper sticker is one of the more interesting mass-produced bumper stickers adorning vehicles today. There are several reasons for this. First, it is probably an indicator that the driver has a pretty positive attitude toward life. Second, he or she is probably a "dog person"—which is a good thing. And third, it symbolizes that being positive and happy probably trumps being mean and grumpy. Have you ever noticed that dogs often wag their tail at the same time they are barking? So you might conclude that dogs are happy even when they are barking. It is a lesson for all of us—all school trustees and board chairs. Your attitude regarding your responsibilities will determine your success in carrying them out!

The Chair's Top 5 Responsibilities

Independent and faith-based school board chairs have numerous responsibilities, and these are often described and debated in numerous books, articles, blogs, online discussions, etc. Perhaps most, if not all, are important contributions. However, the single factor that overcomes all others is to have a great relationship with the head of school. In the absence of this, the school is likely to struggle to realize the full potential of its mission and vision. Given this issue's importance as the pretext for this topic, what then constitutes the board chair's five most important responsibilities?

1. Encourage the Board to Work Together

The idea of the board of trustees working together for the good of the school should be a given. Unfortunately, the reality is often very different. Politics, egos, agendas, conflicts of interest, and ongoing disagreements get in the way of working together. One of the chair's responsibilities is to bring order out of this chaos and remind all board members why they are there—to govern in such a way as to act in the best interest of the school. Differences of opinion? Certainly they are not only a fact of life, but may result in a board making the best decision. Working together, however, will result in what is best about serving on a board of trustees.

2. Insist That Interactions and Relationships Be Not Only Civil But Also Positive

This includes having a positive attitude even when disagreements arise. Our society has gone from a mentality of "reasonable people can disagree" to "let's trash and demonize anyone who disagrees with me" mentality. (Thus, the need for the "wag more, bark less" reminder.) Why has this happened? Is it a reflection of the attitude and rancor that seems to be the way many elected officials behave? Are there other contributing factors? We seem to have forgotten that we have much more in common than different—yet we focus too much on the differences. This attitude will *not* serve the school well but will create a spirit of divisiveness that surely leads to a stalemate. The board chair must navigate through this, set the tone, and have the highest expectations for all members. The chair must articulate the power of positive teamwork as the most reasonable and appropriate way to move forward.

3. Position the Head of School as a Leader Worthy of Respect and Trust

The board chair and the head must be a team and must work together for the good of the school. The chair has to be responsible for insuring that all trustees see the head as a person whom they respect—an individual they believe has the leadership skills needed to make a positive impact. The chair should demonstrate to all trustees that the head exhibits character and integrity, and that he or she is worthy of the trustees' collective and individual support. And the head provides the leadership needed to serve in the top administrative and management role. Not a "mutual admiration society," but rather a genuine sense of working together to communicate this is a compelling shared vision for the school's future. Different roles and responsibilities, but united in outcome and how best to move forward.

4. Ensure That the Board Focuses on Core Responsibilities of Mission, Strategy, Policy, and Planning

The word *micromanaging* (more on this in number 5 below) has almost become a code for school and refers to meddling into areas that are the responsibility of the head of school and his or her leadership team. It occurs so often we have almost become numb to its impact. One of the most fundamental misuses of a board's responsibility is to forget why they are the Board and what their responsibilities include. There is a process that if followed can mean great things. The magic is in the process that the board is educated and trained as to their unique role and the value in that role for the school. Why is it that boards occasionally decide they should *run* the school, which inevitably leads to the *ruin* of the school? When the board insert that *I*, they make a huge mistake! If the board believes there is an absence in leadership, then the members should address that situation rather than try to involve themselves in operational matters. The board's role is strategic, not day to day. The chair must be the cheerleader for insuring that the focus stays on the issues the members are charged with fulfilling.

5. Resist Every Temptation to Meddle or Micromanage Any Member of the Senior Staff.

Certain levels of communication are needed as a part of the structure of the school. Board and staff are often a part of the committee structure and an exchange of ideas in this arena is encouraged. However, there are too many examples of board members going beyond this and using their role of trustee to intimidate and in some cases bully or threaten staff members. Sometimes this behavior is intentional while often it stems from a lack of understanding of roles and responsibilities. This is totally inappropriate and unethical. Almost without fail, the trustee will claim to be innocent and simply misunderstood. This is when the chair is obligated to establish the boundaries of interaction and communication. The head is not in a position to effectively handle this matter because the trustees are the body they report to. It is the chair who must communicate with clarity and purpose as to what is acceptable.

* * *

Being the board chair is a challenging task. However, with this level of leadership comes the responsibility to lead! And that may mean taking a stand and making difficult decisions in order to do what is best for the school *and* supporting the head of school when that is the action required. The challenges are great but the rewards are even greater. This is the type of leadership every board should require of its chair. Having the right leader with the right attitude is a "game changer." Can board chairs wag and bark at the same time? In other words, can they be both positive while sometimes having to be tough on their trustee peers? Wagging more, barking less—not a bad philosophy. We need more bumper stickers with that message!

CASE STORY #8
Undermining the Head of School

The issue was clear. The decision had been made. Yet, that was not the end of it. It was controversial—difficult decisions often are. And controversy brings with it opinions, unwelcome gossip, and speculation. Such is the nature of schools that work with young people—who have parents!

A student was expelled for a major honor code violation. The student handbook was crystal clear regarding the violation—expulsion with no possibility to return. The administration took the appropriate steps, and the student was removed from the school. Almost immediately the student's parents began to lobby for appeal and reinstatement. The parents went to the head of the school, various faculty members, even alumni to lobby on behalf of their student. On each of these occasions, the individuals were informed that the administration had made a decision which would not be reversed.

This went on for months. Each attempt was politely rebuffed. The parents would simply not retreat from their efforts to have their child accepted back into the school. Eventually the parents contacted the chair of the board of trustees. The head of the school was stunned to learn that the chair of the board had agreed to have lunch with the unsatisfied parents! The chair was fully aware from the very beginning of the action taken by the school. The chair was also aware of the repeated attempts on the part of the parents to have their student return to the school.

The chair of the board contacted the head of the school to inform the head that they had agreed to meet and listen to the parents on this matter. The head tried, without success, to explain to the chair that it was not appropriate to give an audience to the parents when a decision had been made months earlier. The chair angrily responded that he would have lunch with whomever he chose and that it was, in his opinion, altogether appropriate to hear them out. The head could not believe the chair had this attitude and had been so defensive. The head requested that the chair share with him the content of the conversation. The chair declined and the head never learned the outcome of their conversation. Fortunately, the chair did not make any move to have the student reinstated.

Questions for Discussion:

1. *Are there circumstances in which a student should be removed from an independent or faith-based school?*
2. *Does it appear that the school took the appropriate action? Why? Why not?*
3. *Could the school have handled the decision and aftermath differently? How?*
4. *When contacted by the parents, did the chair respond appropriately?*
5. *Briefly describe the presence or lack of presence of the following characteristics:*
   - *Collaboration*
   - *Communication*
   - *Trust*
   - *Respect*
   - *Support*
   - *Attitude*
6. *What could the head have done differently?*
7. *What should the chair of the board have done differently?*
8. *What does this incident say about the head and the chair's relationship?*

Chapter Nine

◆

Defining the Culture of the Board: What Should Be Valued and Why

It is true that independent schools have numerous overlapping similarities. At the same time, there are distinct differences. One thing is certain for every school regardless of its size (enrollment), number of grade levels, mission statements, or areas of emphasis: each school has a unique culture. What are the school's values, traditions, customs, philosophy of education, beliefs, and attitudes? Through these various characteristics, the school can begin to define its uniqueness. From a value proposition perspective, what is the "value added" that makes the school stand out to students and families considering one school versus another?

Just as a school has a unique culture so does the school's governing board. Given the nature of the board's work, how do the members view their role, and what is their attitude and behavior in carrying out their responsibilities? The questions posed here strongly suggest the temperament or mood of the board. They go to the core of how those on the board treat their fellow board members, faculty and staff, and head of school.

- What expectations regarding the work of the board have been shared with me?
- What are my expectations and on what are they based?
- How do I view my role of serving on the board?
- What is my attitude toward the work that is before us?
- What is my relationship with the other members of the board?
- As a member of the board, what is my relationship with the school's faculty and staff? With the head of school?
- How important is the board chair in defining what the culture of the board should be?

These questions, and many others, suggest that board culture has much to do with board effectiveness. And board effectiveness is in direct correlation to school effectiveness.

What is meant by serving on the board?

We often hear the phrase, "serving on the board." But what does that really mean? In too many school board rooms, the focus has shifted from "As a trustee, how can I best serve and meet the needs of the board and the school" to "As a corporate leader, others should always listen to what I have to say because I'm a powerful person and know more than anyone else." An exaggeration? Perhaps, but there is a clear and troubling cultural shift moving people away from service, humility, and a desire to help and towards ego, power, and an "it's all about me" attitude The time has come to remind board members that the expectation as a board of trustees is to *serve* on the board and *serve* the school. A healthy and productive board consists of members who park their egos, inappropriate agendas, and power trips at the board room door.

Board members who are current parents have a unique relationship with the school's parent body and the board.

One of the defining characteristics of almost every independent and faith-based school is having current parents serve on the governing board. It is the ultimate two-edged sword. On the one hand, these board parents willingly serve and strive to be a positive influence and are seeking to be a best practices trustee. On the other hand, there are board parents who come with agendas, whose self-interests and power-seeking methods define their tenure. Such board members believe that they represent parents who are in search of a voice, people who do not necessarily see the greater good, but who want to know what's in it for them and their children. Having parents on the board is often a gratifying and rewarding experience, but it can occasionally be a nightmare for other trustees and the head of school. What does the board's culture have to do with this issue? What kind of governing board does the school desire? One that is moving forward strategically and one that always places students and faculty at the center of the conversation?

This is also about leadership and clearly articulating expectations. The board chair as well as the committee on trustees must continually educate current parents who are trustees regarding what the board values and why. The value proposition for these board members includes how these trustees relate and communicate with the school's parent body, and accordingly, how these trustees' behavior impacts board conversations and decisions. It is perhaps too great a challenge to educate all parents about what this relationship should look like. It is altogether a different matter to educate board members regarding how this relationship works in the best interest of all involved.

As a board member, you have numerous responsibilities to be the best trustee possible. Not included in those responsibilities is solving problems parents may have with the school.

Absent ongoing board education, many trustees believe that part of their role is to be a problem solver for parents. This is not the case. There are many valid situations in which a parent will have a concern or issue with a teacher, coach, staff member, and even another parent. Such scenarios are not unusual. However, when parents believe their problems should be taken directly to a board member who may be a fellow parent, even a good friend, the board's responsibility and cultural norm is to express to these parents that there is another path they should pursue for the resolution to their issue.

As a board member, your agenda lists one item: How can I serve in a way that is helpful, meaningful, and strategic?

Having an agenda that is based on a trustee's strengths, passions, and particular interest is not only acceptable but should be encouraged. In fact, these characteristics may have much to do with why a trustee was considered. The problem occurs when board members take their agenda to a harmful place, believing they know better than anyone else about whatever their interest happens to be. These trustees have lost the ability to listen because they are on a power trip under the illusion that they know best and certainly more than anyone else on the board. This is dangerous territory. Ultimately, it is the agreed upon strategic direction that must take precedent over the personal priorities of one or a few trustees. If this scenario is allowed to play out it potentially can be a distraction to the board, the head of school, as well as faculty and staff. The board's leadership should remind new trustees—and all trustees, for that matter—that the agenda is defined by the mission and vision of the school as well as by the strategic plan, a process that has led to its adoption by the board of trustees.

The designated boardroom is always the appropriate location for the board meeting—not the parking lot, the car-rider line, or the bathroom.

There is little that more distinctly defines board culture than this problem. And make no mistake, this is a real problem for far too many boards. It happens when board leadership has lost control and allows or tolerates board-related discussions to take place outside of board or sanctioned committee meetings. There are numerous reasons why this type of behavior is inappropriate, unethical, and potentially illegal. Topping the list of concerns are matters of trust, teamwork, and confidentiality. Like every other potential issue, this will define a board's culture in troubling ways. It must be discussed with all prospective trustees. One thing the committee on trustees should never do is assume that everyone understands that this is unacceptable conduct.

The school's board of trustees functions best as a team, and this aspect of teamwork is diminished when a board member goes rogue and singles out select trustees, parents, or alumni to have a casual conversation with regarding a board issue. The board member may cry foul and say, "I was only trying to get input from a different perspective," but this failure to grasp the value of teamwork may become a more serious matter if he or she ends up sharing confidential information with someone who is not a trustee. Someone, of course, who is in no way bound to confidentiality and who may decide to share this on social media. The consequences might be devastating. The safest and most prudent course of action is to confine board discussions to the officially sanctioned board meeting or committee meeting. Whether well-intentioned or mean-spirited, the board must place the highest possible value on trust, teamwork, and confidentiality. These traits will always serve the board well. Working together for what is in the best interest of the school should always be the defining priority, never taken for granted, and trumps whatever else the board might consider essential.

Knowing everything and telling everything are two different things.

Confidentiality is one of the most important qualities a governing board can have. Yet it is often ignored, misunderstood, or abused above all the responsibilities of a school's board. It should be a fundamental aspect of a board's culture, and yet it is given lip service. To be sure, it is a fundamental responsibility of the independent school's board. The question then becomes, do we believe it is important, and what are the consequences if this responsibility is ignored by one or more trustees? Behavior defines culture and culture defines values. If the board is aware of the problem and chooses to ignore it, that says something very clear and troubling about the board and its leadership. If, on the other hand, the board takes a stand and makes it clear by example that breaking confidentiality is not acceptable and may result in removal of the board member, then there is greater likelihood that board members will take this responsibility seriously and pause before violating confidentiality.

The question then becomes, what can be shared and with whom can it be shared? All board discussions, interactions, and communication should be kept in strictest confidence. Actions, decisions, and policies voted on or otherwise adopted by the board may be shared as long as the board determines the method, timing, and language of such announcements. The board chair or his or her designee should be the only spokesperson for the board. All questions should be referred to the chair unless other instructions override this decision.

Board members will sometimes raise the question of what can be shared with a spouse. The safest and surest path is to share board information with no one, including a spouse. This can be a challenge for some couples in certain circumstances. However, such a strategy protects the spouse from being confronted with questions when he or she can say with all candor, "I don't have knowledge or information about what you are asking me."

As a trustee, you do not represent the constituency from which you come.

Independent schools, or Christian schools, or most other types of private schools have self-perpetuating boards, meaning that the committee on trustees makes the initial determination as to who should be considered for board service. It is then the responsibility of the full board to vote on all prospective trustees being considered. This process is not a popular election as most public school boards are established to represent a specific school district within a particular area. Because most of us have some awareness of this process, we are sometimes confused by how the process of naming independent school board members and that of public school board members is a vastly different method of operation.

An independent school board's members are identified and appointed because of their knowledge, skills, expertise, and willingness to support the school. Such trustees may be addressing a demographic need or may be filling a need of one of the school's constituencies—parent, alumni, grandparent, etc. These trustees are present on their own merits and do not act or vote on their perception of what is popular with parents, alumni, or any other group.

The board has one employee—the head of school.

The purpose of this statement goes directly to how the organizational chart is designed and, more importantly, looks at the behavior, attitude, and actions of individual trustees. In theory, most trustees understand what this means. Actual practice is often a very different matter. This repeatedly appears when parents who are also members of the board have either forgotten or have failed to grasp the difference between a parent issue and a board issue. Trustees must never fail to remember that every member of the faculty and staff either directly or indirectly reports to the head of school—not to the board nor to any member of the board of trustees. Let there be no confusion in that regard. Parents who also happen to serve on the board are well within their rights to communicate with a teacher, coach, or staff member regarding a situation involving their student. However, these same parents are not to communicate with a teacher, coach, or staff member regarding a governance-related issue. It is confusing and potentially intimidating for a parent trustee to communicate with a teacher about any topic that would give the appearance of having something to do with the work of the board. Teachers do not answer to board members—even if those members are parents, alumni, grandparents, or any other constituency of the school.

Should the board chair become aware of this type of behavior, he or she must act on it immediately. This is a serious matter that the board must take seriously and not allow to become acceptable or the norm. The board chair can determine how best to address this. But some form of ongoing education, such as a retreat, is one way. Another is to make this topic part of the orientation for new trustees so they are made aware when beginning their term of office.

Partnership between the head and board should define their work together and the accompanying behavior that goes along with it.

This is a simple idea that can have such an impact on schools. The idea is that we are all working together to enhance and advance the school. In other words, the key to maximizing effectiveness is this partnership quality that will make such a positive difference on the school's mission, vision, and strategic objectives. And yet schools get bogged down in the politics of governance, leadership, and management. Before you know it, everyone has lost sight of the objective and becomes focused on trivial and meaningless distractions. It will ultimately cause damage to the school, and the students will suffer the most. Focus on hiring the best possible head of school with the ensuing behavior built on trust and support, encouraging him or her at every turn. Let this simple idea prevail and the results will speak for themselves.

Questions to consider: When are you a trustee and when are you not? Does the head report to the board, individual trustees, or both? How can the board chair ensure the board's behavior reflects best practices?

There is confusion and misunderstanding when it comes to this issue. When is it appropriate to wear the trustee hat and when is it not? Absent proper board education on this matter, it is somewhat easy for this to be a confusing issue. On the other hand, the answer is straightforward. A trustee is a trustee when the board is holding regularly scheduled or special called meetings of the board. This includes all official board committee meetings. You are not a trustee when standing in the parking lot following the board meeting. You are not a trustee when attending a school event. Nor are you a trustee when walking in the mall or standing in line at the grocery store. You have no authority as an individual board member. Nor do you have authority to speak representing the board.

The head of school does not report to individual board members. Again, this is not always clearly understood or articulated with trustees. Given the statements in the previous paragraph, the concept of the head reporting or somehow answering to individual trustees is an erroneous one. As an individual, the board member has no authority. This often plays out as trustees are unaware of how this works. A board member calling the head wanting information about a disciplinary issue, for example, would only be proper if the incident in question pertained to his or her child. Trust is an important aspect of this issue and the board member must recognize that he or she is putting the head on the spot by requesting information that has no bearing on the governance of the school.

The head does report to the board or a board committee in the context of a board or board committee meeting. And, for clarity as well as logistically, the head does report to the board chair; the two must work in genuine partnership to ensure governance and leadership effectiveness. The board chair has the unmistakable responsibility to shape how the board conducts itself when it comes to this issue. Trustees will take their que as to what behavior is acceptable based in large part on how the chair conducts himself or herself. To be certain, the chair must realize that attitude and behavior directly impact actions.

Why does this matter? Independent and faith-based schools play a significant role in the delivery of educating students around the world. The stakes are high to get it right because these schools are in the business of not only educating students, but changing lives and preparing leaders who will make a difference. Healthy boards will help secure a future that will lead to a better world.

CASE STORY #9
Supporting the New Head of School

Claire was excited about the head of school search she was about to embark upon. Following a successful career as a head of school, she joined a well-respected search firm focusing on searches for all types of independent schools. She knew that her new assignment would present some unique challenges but she was confident that with a thorough process and an excellent relationship with the search committee, board of trustees, and current head of school, she could lead a search that would result in the appointment of the best possible head of school.

The challenge she faced was that in Riverview Academy's thirty-five year history the school had only had one head of school. Now he was retiring and the search committee had engaged Claire's firm to conduct the search for the school's second head of school in thirty-five years. She knew the retiring head and knew he was a man deep faith, impeccable integrity, and most of all was anxious for the school to thrive after he was gone. One of the interesting aspects of the search was that the search committee wanted Richard, the current head, to be an ex-officio member of the committee. While Claire was concerned, she knew Richard and was confident that he could be an asset on the committee.

Claire met with the search committee and described the process that the search committee would need to follow over the next several months in order to identify the best possible candidate to be the head of Riverview. Above all, she encouraged the committee to trust the process, trust her, and that if they worked together and followed her counsel an appropriate candidate pool would emerge.

All head searches are unique, but the search at Riverview had two issues that would surface as potential roadblocks to a successful outcome. One, Claire knew that anyone following the founding head would face a range of challenges that might undermine his or her ability to lead. Two, having the founding head on the search committee. This would be a problem if the search committee and board members were not mature enough to handle the search objectively. As Claire had worked with Riverview in the past, she knew from her experience that the board had not always been what she thought of as a best-practices board. However, the chair of the board was the chair of the search committee, and Claire was impressed with his ability to lead the process.

As the process unfolded, there were issues that she communicated to the search committee numerous times, issues that she felt were vital for the search to reveal the best candidate. She realized that if these issues were not adhered to, the candidate might have a difficult time navigating the political aspects that come along with every new head of school. To Claire these points were non-negotiable:

1. The founding head of school could, in no way, interfere with or be present during the transition year.
2. The new head must be given full authority without interference or input (unless requested by the new head) to lead the school in the manner he or she thought best.
3. The chair of the search committee must remain as the chair of the board for a minimum of one year after the new head arrives—longer if at all possible.
4. The members of the search committee must also remain on the board not less than a year after the new head arrives on campus.

5. The full board must agree to hold a retreat with the new head with Claire facilitating the retreat. The purpose would be to get to know the new head, begin to establish critical relationships, and set strategic goals for the next year or two.

6. Perhaps most essential, when the search committee made its recommendation to the full board for approval, both the search committee and the full board must be unanimous in their support of the new head. Any second-guessing or split vote could potentially lead to disaster and a short tenure for the head.

As the search progressed, these issues were communicated and documented to the search committee. The search process produced about forty candidates for the position. As with most searches, there were a number of candidates that simply were not an appropriate fit for the school. Claire had done extensive background work including contacting a number of candidates she thought would be a great fit as the search profile articulated.

Over time and after numerous meetings and conversations, Claire and the search committee identified five excellent candidates who would be the semi-finalists for the position. The candidates were geographically diverse and included three men and two women. Claire felt very good about the pool and believed any of the five could do the job effectively. The interviews went well, and the search committee had a difficult challenge narrowing the search from five candidates to three. The search committee was, however, confident that the search process would uncover a new head of school.

The three finalists came to campus for two full days of interviews and meetings with various constituencies of the school. All did well under circumstances designed to reveal skills such as leadership and character and abilities demonstrating a capacity to perform under pressure. Following the interviews, the search committee came together to discuss, evaluate, and make a recommendation to the full board. While the discussion was lengthy and the decision difficult, the search committee was confident in their selection and prepared to make a recommendation to the board.

After a six months search, the committee met with the board. There was some discussion from the board, but in the end, the board accepted the recommendation of the search committee. Claire noted that while the vote had been unanimous, there seemed to be a lack of shared enthusiasm among board members. It was almost as if the board did not fully trust the process. A few trustees seemed to have a wish list in their minds and were not completely convinced the new head met their expectations. Claire did not realize it at the time, but this may have been the beginning of the end.

On March 1, Spencer was appointed the new head of school with a start date of the following July 1. This came with the usual publicity and fanfare associated with the completion of the search process. Claire believed the best candidate had been selected and wrapped up her duties hopeful that the board would abide by the six guiding principles she had made clear were mandatory.

Spencer arrived in July and all seemed to go well initially. It wasn't long before concerns surfaced that made Claire feel uneasy as to where this might lead. First, the chair of the search committee refused to stay on for an additional term as chair of the board. He had decided he had been chair long enough and did not believe being chair would make any difference to the new head. He agreed to stay on as a member of the board. Second, every member of the search committee left the board within the first year of Spencer's arrival. Third, no retreat was held as it was deemed to be too time-consuming and an unnecessary step in Spencer's transition. Fourth, the board had negotiated with the founding head that he could stay on at the school in a limited capacity and have an office at the school. And finally, Claire was not sure the board was unanimous in its support for Spencer, and this revealed itself in a very unfortunate way about a year into Spencer's tenure as head.

One of the changes that Spencer felt was necessary was a change in the lower school leadership position. Following months of discussion, the lower school principal agreed to step down creating the opportunity to bring in an interim while conducting a search for a new lower school head. Spencer was put in an awkward position when one of the board members approached him about appointing the board member's spouse as the interim principal. Spencer's first thought was this is a bad idea and counter to best practices. The conflict of interest implications were obvious. The only way this could work is if the board member stepped down from the board. This did not happen, and Spencer felt obligated to appoint the spouse of his board member. In the meantime, Spencer worked on the position description for the new lower school principal and amended the description in such a way to add duties that the former principal did not have. Although not his intent, he suspected that the interim principal might not have the necessary skills as well. Because of the adjusted position description, the board member's spouse did not apply for the position. The board member was convinced that Spencer had intentionally altered the description as to eliminate his wife from consideration. This was not Spencer's intent.

Ultimately a new principal was hired. The board member could not get beyond the issue in his mind that Spencer had done all of this intentionally in order to disqualify his wife. He began to make this an issue in board meetings as well as outside board meetings. The new board chair was a weak leader and unable to confront the board member to let him know his behavior was inappropriate and unethical. It didn't take long for this board member to influence others to his way of thinking. The situation disintegrated into an ugly confrontation. Spencer went back to Claire for guidance and she believed Spencer was in jeopardy of not only losing the confidence of certain members of the board but possibly losing his job. She advised him to encourage the chair of the board to hold a retreat to discuss issues that should have been addressed at the time Spencer was hired. She feared, however, that because of the absence of effective leadership on the part of the board, it was too late and Spencer's tenure was in trouble.

The chair refused to hold a retreat and refused to discipline the board member whose behavior had been completely inappropriate regarding the appointment of his wife to an administrative position at the school. Two months into Spencer's second year as head of school, the board asked him to resign effective immediately. To add insult to injury they did not intend to compensate him according to the terms of his contract. In the end, he had to retain an attorney to force the board to do the right thing and compensate him for the remainder of his contract. Needless to say, Spencer was devastated but resolved to move forward, although knowing he would likely be reluctant to consider another head's position. Eventually, perhaps. Following his dismissal, the weak board chair resigned. He was replaced by the board member who had created this situation by insisting his spouse be the lower school principal.

Questions for Discussion

1. *What could Claire have done differently to better prepare the board for the head transition?*
2. *Should she have done more about the warning signs that she knew from experience existed?*
3. *What should have the founding head done differently?*
4. *Succession is always difficult. What were the issues at Riverview Academy?*
5. *The board is dysfunctional. What will happen with the next search?*
6. *Why is this story all too common among all types of independent schools?*

CASE STORY #10
The New Board Chair

The e-mail simply said, "It's urgent. I need to see you now." Natalie had been the chair of the board of Mooreland School for less than two months, although she had served on the board for several years. She read this second message and was confused about why she was receiving an e-mail directly from a member of the faculty. This didn't seem right, but she was not sure why. In the first e-mail, Dana had stated the she was very upset that the textbook for next year's class had been changed and approved without her input. She had been a long-standing member of the faculty and felt very strongly that such a decision should not have been made without consulting her. She had spoken with the upper school principal and the head of school. Both had informed her that a combination of timing, plus the two school leaders thought the new text was an improvement over what was currently being used at Mooreland, had led to the decision.

Natalie was unsure how to proceed with the demanding faculty member. She contacted the board's vice chair, Scott, and, not knowing exactly what to do, they agreed to meet with Dana. The meeting was arranged and soon after the three sat down for a conversation about the issue of changing text books—the chair of the board, the vice chair, and a member of the school's faculty met to discuss textbooks. Natalie began by asking if Dana had spoken with the principal and head of school about this matter. Dana indicated that she had and was told why the decision was made and the process by which the decision was made. Dana was also informed that decisions like this were part of the responsibility of being the upper school principal and head of school. She was unclear whether or not this was an actual school policy or rather a process the head of school claimed had occurred numerous times during her tenure as head of school. Both Natalie and Scott listened to Dana's argument and agreed they would meet with the head of school as soon as possible.

A few days later, Natalie and Scott met with Brenda, who had been head of Mooreland for about ten years. From the outset of the meeting, Brenda was extremely upset with Natalie and Scott for coming to her on what clearly in her mind was an academic, school operational issue—not an issue that involved board chair and vice chair intervention. She explained she had met with Dana, enlightened her as to why and how the decision was made and, as far as she was concerned, that was the end of it. Brenda never dreamed that Dana would then go the chair of the board to complain about an issue such as this.

During the meeting, Natalie confessed that she was unclear about her role in this matter and was simply trying to resolve a conflict between the head, the principal, and a member of the faculty. Brenda took exception to this and in rather unsympathetic terms made it clear how disappointed she was in the actions of the chair and vice chair. In all her years as head of school she had never had the chair of the board discuss such an issue with her. Brenda further stated that, to her, the matter was concluded and nothing further needed to be done. Natalie and Scott didn't know what to make of the conversation. Brenda was not rude but she was direct and additional discussion was unnecessary.

Following the meeting Natalie was clearly rattled by the turn of events and was not sure what to think or do next. Had she been wrong to meet the faculty member? Soon after she contacted someone she knew about who had extensive experience in working with independent school boards. For Natalie, that phone call was not an especially pleasant one. Michael, who had been a head of school and had years of experience working with schools and boards was quite surprised to hear the story as Natalie shared all the details in order to learn what his reaction would be. Michael's immediate reaction was to thank Natalie for her judgement in trying to learn what best practices would indicate in such a situation as this. Michael then proceeded to thoughtfully share his concerns for the events that Natalie had conveyed to him. He shared the following:

- The most important best practices principle that Natalie had failed to understand is that the board has only one employee and that is the head of school.
- Every member of the faculty and staff reports either directly or indirectly to the head of school.
- A member of the faculty going directly to the board chair without informing and seeking permission from the head was an act of insubordination.
- The board chair should not have agreed to meet with the faculty member but should have immediately contacted the head of school and informed her of what had taken place.
- The board chair and the entire board should never involve themselves in operational issues. They have hired the head of school for the operation and management of the school.
- An overreach such as this demonstrates a significant lack of trust in the leadership of the head of school.
- The board should, as soon as possible, hold a retreat to discuss appropriate roles and responsibilities as a way to measure and ensure best practices.

Natalie recognized she had stepped into an area that was not her place to do so. She recognized there was more to being the board chair than she realized. And there was much she needed to learn to be as effective as possible. Mooreland's future was at stake!

Questions for Discussion

1. *Because Natalie was uncertain about this issue, why didn't she contact Michael before responding to Dana's insisting on a meeting?*
2. *What does this story reveal about the necessity of ongoing board education?*
3. *What should Natalie do regarding further communication with the faculty member?*
4. *What would bring closure to this matter?*
5. *Why are individuals like Michael so helpful in situations like this?*

Chapter Ten

◆

Characteristics and Skills Necessary for Success

There is a familiar expression that applies to the manner and process of adding members to the school's board of trustees: "If you do what you have always done, then you will get what you have always gotten." Simply stated, the board must look for other types or categories of prospective members—those who will possess the characteristics needed for the best in volunteer leadership.

Seven Types of Board Members to Consider

The committee on trustees and any others on the board who have a responsibility to secure new members of the board should consider these seven "types" of leaders:

1. Individuals who will work and accept both individual and team responsibilities.

Attracting board members to the school is one thing; but quite another is attracting individuals who will willingly accept the responsibilities of the work required in making a personal, individual commitment as well as embracing the idea that they are part of a team of trustees who must speak with one voice. This must be clearly communicated during the trustee recruiting process.

2. Well-known and respected individuals whose names, reputations, and credibility would add a dimension to the school not currently available.

Every person named to the board must bring something that adds value to the board and therefore to the school. Individuals who demonstrate character and integrity and have the skills needed should always make the short list. Independent schools should look for name recognition—but there is much more to it than that. It will be difficult to attract someone simply because they are well known. Typically, schools benefit if the person is well known *and* has an interest and connection to the school's mission and vision.

> NOTE: *There are strategic ways in which the school can identify and attract individuals who are not currently aware of what you do. One example is to establish a "board of visitors" as a way in which to engage such individuals without the responsibilities required of board members.*

3. Individuals who are considered to be "on their way up" in the community but are not yet overcommitted.

Many communities all across the country have initiated programs that identify young leaders who are beginning to demonstrate an interest in giving back and making a difference in their communities through their success or potential. One such organization is the Young Leaders Council. Its purpose is to work with young leaders (approximately twenty-five to forty years in age) and train them to understand what is involved in being an excellent board member. This is one example among many. Schools have a unique opportunity to attract these "up-and-comers" who have the potential to be outstanding board members. The downside is that they may not be in a position to make a significant financial commitment. But that ability to give may come, and there are other contributions they can make immediately. This is a constituency easily overlooked. The smart, strategic school will carefully consider opportunities to add this category of board member.

4. Well-positioned community leaders who will contribute "time, talent, and/or treasure," or leaders who will "give and get."

While this is easier for the well-known or long-established school, any school can attract these individuals to your board. First, to do so it must be a strategic priority. In other words, you must be intentional and set this as a goal for the board and be willing to be evaluated on it. Tactically, it probably starts with your current board members. Do you have someone, or more than one person, who is in such a position and has the clout and desire to assist in attracting others who fall into this category? If so, work with them to connect who they know with the school—other board members as well as senior administrative leadership.

The whole *work, wealth, wisdom* and *time, talent, treasure* discussion regarding board responsibilities has become something of an overused cliché. But it does not make these skills any less valid or necessary. And it is certainly a starting point of a dialogue when looking for skills needed to enhance the performance of the board.

5. Active, involved, and mature young leaders.

Maturity is a character trait often lacking in the young. However, maturity coupled with activity within young people who are involved in their communities is the beginning of excellent board members. The challenge is to convince this type of individual to join your ranks. The first step is *identification*—be intentional as to whom you want. The second step is *information*—take the steps necessary to provide information that will uncover their level of interest. The third step is *involvement*—creating the opportunities to learn more about their potential interest as well as understanding of the school's mission and vision will equip board recruiters with valuable evidence as to what kind of trustee the person is likely to become.

6. Upper-level and middle-level managers of area corporations.

All too often schools try to reach too high in the hierarchy of a business or corporation when seeking new board members. In fact, it may not be the CEO or the president that is the best fit but rather someone in upper- or middle-level management. This issue is made more challenging if the person you seek has no definable connection to your school. There are often very talented people at these levels who are looking for opportunities to validate their role in the company by making a commitment to the school and in the community. They understand that giving back creates circumstances for moving up.

7. Active spouses, sons, and daughters of well-established leaders in the school community.

This category of prospective board member should be near the top of your list to consider. Often overlooked, they have enormous potential for their own skills but also for their connections and associations with family members who are in a position to significantly impact the school. A wealthy and influential father can be a very grateful donor when his daughter is asked to be on the board!

Four Helpful Skills of Board Members

There are also certain skills that you should look for in prospective board members. These include:

1. Cultivate or develop donors and solicit gifts for the school.

As mentioned in Chapter 12, this skill is thought to be a given. Don't believe it—be very intentional regarding expectations. If this skill is a board priority then act accordingly and communicate this expectation with prospective board members as well as current ones.

2. Cultivate and recruit board members and other volunteer leaders.

It is the responsibility of good board members to seek out and find other good members to help perpetuate the work the current board is doing. An ability and willingness to understand why this is important should either be clear or made clear to the board member. The continuous flow of individuals who are prepared to serve with distinction must always be an important priority. It is the very fabric of what continuity is all about.

3. Understand the financial position of the organization.

We all know that the board has the responsibility for the financial well-being of the school. It is necessary and appropriate that board members grasp issues that relate to the budget, assets, endowment investment, and all matters financial. Having said that, the board and the school are more than this. Additional perspectives are needed to provide balance. Having a core group that is well versed in the financial position is vital to sustainability.

4. Continually learn about programs of the organization.

While mission, vision, strategy, and planning are at the forefront of what the board is accountable for overseeing, they should also be informed about the programs (academic, arts, athletics, cocurricular) of the school. Much of this should jointly be accomplished through efforts of the head of school and the board chair to ensure that all board members are well acquainted with school objectives and priorities.

Additional Skills Useful to the School

In addition to the list above, these are some general skills that will always prove to be vital to the health of any independent or faith-based school:

1. Ability to listen, analyze, and think clearly and creatively.

Listening skills are often overlooked but badly needed. Part of effective listening skills is understanding and working from the idea that "it's not all about me." This is a valuable perspective, and it suggests an attitude of teamwork, collaboration, and trust.

2. Ability to work with people individually and in groups.

Working well with others includes the ability to work together for common goals, to work as a team, find consensus, and to compromise when appropriate.

3. Willingness to prepare for and participate in committee meetings.

Service on the board clearly means active involvement and participation. Showing up for board meetings is merely the first step. Engaging in the real work requires serving on committees as needed.

4. Contribute personal resources in a generous way, suggesting board membership is a philanthropic priority during the time of active involvement and service.

Giving as generously as one is able suggests that during the time on the board the school is unquestionably a philanthropic priority. There should be a distinction made between serving on a school's board and having any other kind of relationship. Take, for example, your alma mater. As an alumnus or alumna of your school, you may be a donor depending on numerous factors, chief among them the experience you had as a student and the impact the school has had on your life and career. When you agree to serve as a trustee of that school, your relationship changes dramatically and the school becomes more central to your volunteer commitments. Your giving should therefore align with your commitment and thus become a financial priority to the best of your capacity.

5. Opening doors in the community is beneficial to the organization.

By utilizing your sphere of influence, it is incumbent to provide introductions and access where it will have the most impact for the school. For this very reason is part of why someone is asked to serve on the board.

CASE STORY #11
The Head's Role in Trustee Selection

In a visit with a head of school we began a conversation about governance. He had been the head of this school for four years and was still working for/with the board chair when he was appointed. Had there been a transition to someone new in that role?

One of the most critical issues for a school is the ability to successfully navigate the transition from the chair in place when a new head of school is appointed to a new chair. This is a place ripe for a breakdown in the relationship between the head, board, and board chair.

A new chair of the board had been appointed. During the ensuing discussion, he described almost the ideal scenario about how this transition can most effectively occur. When this happens the school and ultimately the students, parents, alumni, faculty, staff, *and* board members will benefit from the positive environment that will result.

He shared that when it was time to appoint a new chair, he, the head of school, was not only included in the discussion about who should be the next chair, he was given the opportunity to express any concerns regarding anyone being considered. In addition, he was given veto power over anyone he deemed unqualified for the position. During the course of our conversation he revealed that he had expressed serious concerns over two of the prospective candidates because he possessed knowledge that could have blossomed into a major problem.

There are seven essential characteristics that must be in place for the head and board chair to work effectively. This remarkable episode suggests the presence of all seven:

1. *Communication and Collaboration.* The ability to candidly discuss the needs of the school in such a way that demonstrates a desire to do what is right and ensure what is best takes precedence.
2. *Respect.* Mutual respect must be present to create an environment in which all relevant issues can be put forward.
3. *Trust.* Trust is necessary to confidently and confidentially debate strengths and weaknesses of those being considered.
4. *Support.* The ability to support the decision of the head is critical to enhancing the relationship.
5. *Shared Vision.* Leadership is the key to every aspect of the school and agreeing on the kind of individual necessary to move forward is essential.
6. *Attitude.* The attitude of everyone involved suggests the positive way in which to approach such a critical decision.
7. *Leadership.* Everything rises and falls with leadership. Select the right person and all things are possible. Make the wrong decision and the wrong leader could have dire consequences for the school as well as the potential for reversal of progress.

Congratulations to this head of school and to his enlightened board who clearly grasp the importance of what a genuine difference leadership can make. His story is encouraging because it provides such a positive example of this process and how it can result in the continuity of effective leadership.

Questions for Discussion

1. *Why do you believe this relationship works?*
2. *What should your bylaws say about board chair succession?*
3. *What advice would you give other independent or faith-based schools about this issue?*
4. *Would different individuals in these roles produce different results?*
5. *Why does succession in leadership matter?*

Chapter Eleven

◆

Structuring the Board
for Success

There are numerous ways for the board to be structured. Many of these unique ways in which the board fulfills its obligation can be found in the language of the bylaws and policies adopted by the board. What best practices and structure result in a significant group of individuals working together to achieve greatness for the school?

Board Manual

The board manual is one of the most useful resources to assist in providing a sense of integration and belonging to individual members of the board. It is important that this document be attractively presented in a loose-leaf notebook binder that is given to each new board member and updated during their time of service on the board of trustees. While a board notebook may seem "old school," there should be a place where such information can succinctly tell the story of the school and provide board members with an overview and outline of the school.

Board manuals should include the following information:

- School's charter
- Bylaws
- Description and brief history of the school
- Schedule of the plan of work for the board
- Roster of board members, officers, committee makeup, and past chairs
- Statement of policies
- Organizational chart
- Current budget
- Copies of publications—magazines, brochures, marketing and development materials
- Schedule of meetings

It is important that the manual be prepared by a collaboration of the committee on trustees, the head of school, and other staff leaders. Each time new trustees are added, the board manual should be updated and distributed to the entire board.

Bylaws and Committee Descriptions

As a 501(c)(3) organization, bylaws are required as documents legally and fundamentally necessary to be a nonprofit independent or faith-based school. Bylaws document how the school is governed. Bylaws may be very detailed or may be very broadly defined. Each school must determine for itself exactly what is included and what is excluded from this document. While bylaws constitute the governing rules of the school, that should not imply that they have to be lengthy or contain more legal jargon than is absolutely necessary. For a more complete look at bylaws and their place in your school, please see Appendixes A, B, and C.

Whether in the bylaws or in some other document of the school, having written descriptions of the responsibilities of each of the standing committees is a very good practice. There are several reasons why this is a good idea including:

- Written committee descriptions demonstrate the school's commitment to providing resources and information that will help trustees understand and perform their duties.
- Written descriptions leave minimal room for misinterpretation as to priorities and needs.
- Written descriptions help prospective and new trustees move promptly to learning about the school and the committee structure.

The Appropriate Size of the Board

The number of members on the board of trustees has much to do with the history and institutional culture of the school. Most boards have evolved over time to reflect the current nature of the school. It is probably true with many schools that they looked at similar schools to help determine the number of board members. Ultimately the issue of size must be the decision of the board itself. Again, collaboration with the head of school and staff leadership is a key in reviewing these issues.

Problems will certainly surface if the board becomes too large or too small. When a board becomes too large it often creates an "inner" board. This inner board may be formalized like the executive committee, or may be a less structured group that becomes a functioning center of control.

The board must be large enough, though, to carry out its duties and responsibilities. A board that is too small in number will not be able to carry out the necessary policy guidance and leadership that is vital to the school's mission and vision. If too small it may not be able to accommodate all groups or constituencies that should be represented for decision making. A small board may also become too closely knit and clannish. And there may be the practical challenge of not having enough to constitute a quorum.

There are several different ways to determine the appropriate size of the board. One is more objective, calculating the number of committees, the number of members per committee, and the number of officers, considering those who will serve on special or ad hoc committees.

It is best for boards to have an uneven number of voting members. While many operate and make most decisions by consensus, there is always the very real possibility of a tie vote on certain issues. If the board does have an even number of members then provision must be made as to how a tie vote will be broken. While boards rarely find themselves in this predicament, it is wise to be aware of the potential problems that could arise.

Tenure

How long someone stays on the board is a matter of interest and concern for all of the board members. There are various discussions and debates that argue for, on the one hand, a prolonged tenure. And there are others that argue for a shorter time of service. The weight, however, suggests that neither extreme constitutes a best practice. The term of service must be long enough to provide all-important continuity of policies and practice, but short enough to secure and ensure continuous freshness of perspective.

There are two resolutions that address this issue. First is the establishment of definite terms of appointment. The second is the limitation of the number of consecutive terms each member may serve. Although these two resolutions are related, they are distinctive.

The argument of no term limits dismisses the larger issue of having fresh perspective and providing more people with the opportunity to be involved and contribute in different ways with the organization.

Many schools have adopted the three-year term of membership with the opportunity to serve a second term, for a total of six years of service. After that, many bylaws state that the person must go off the board for at least one year before being considered again.

Overlapping Terms

Most boards have defined terms for their members with provision for overlapping membership. These defined term limits provide:

- A pattern of beginning and termination points that allows for continuity and for changes in membership
- Built-in motivation for those who want to continue on the board
- An easier plan to build a broader base of support
- A consistent mechanism for removing uninterested, ineffective members from the board

For example, if a board of a school had eighteen members, with three-year term limits, then a typical "class" would include six each year—with some returning for a second term and some beginning a first term.

Limitation of Terms

While it is not universally advisable for volunteer boards to have term limitations, for most boards some kind of term limitation should be seriously considered. The concept is a simple one—

every member of the board should be required to go off the board after serving a consecutive number of terms, usually two or three terms. As stated above, many bylaws written today state that after a set number of terms, the board member may not be considered again until the individual has been off the board for at least one year. Even a particularly valuable board member should step down for some period before being elected again.

Past Board Members

This question almost never fails to arise: What is the most useful way to engage past (former) board members? Many schools do not have a very good answer to this question as they simply allow them to fade into the past. However, there are schools that recognize the value and importance of these individuals and develop very strategic ways to encourage their continual engagement. Some of these ways are more formal than others. The creation of a structure, such as a board of advisors, can be made up exclusively or partly with past board members. Regardless of the manner in which this happens, it is in the school's best interest to keep these past board members involved and engaged.

Selection and Transition of the Board Chair

The chair of the board is an enormously important position in the school. That person's relationship with the entire board and the head of school is critical to living out the mission. No other relationship is as critical as that of the board chair and head. Through the bylaws and the culture of the board, the chair must be carefully selected to ensure that it is someone who possesses qualities of leadership, integrity, responsibility, respect, and support. It is imperative that the chair be an individual who understands the role of the board and is not troubled by the need to restrain or, if necessary, discipline members of the board if they fail to adhere to policies and guidelines.

Another critical component is the manner in which the transition occurs between one board chair and the next. This task should be articulated in the school's bylaws and implemented in the most seamless way possible. The board should avoid extremes in personality and working relationships when choosing the board chair. Working with the board and head should be viewed as a primary responsibility of the chair.

Committee Structure

Of all the aspects of board membership, it is the committee structure and process that is most subject to mock horror and heavy-handed humor. In spite of misconceptions, committees continue to flourish and are an integral part of the volunteer board structure. There are at least three types of committees—standing, special (or ad hoc), and coordinating.

1. *Standing committees* are those that remain in existence indefinitely in order to consider ongoing issues of the board. Such committees are identified in the bylaws and are often accompanied by a description of committee responsibilities. These typically include a budget (or finance) committee, committee on trustees (or governance committee), building/grounds committee, and development committee. The school may also include other standing committees they believe are necessary for unique circumstances.

2. *Special* or *ad hoc committees* are appointed to address a specific situation and then cease to exist once the issue has been resolved. An example might be a search committee that is created to conduct a search for a position

within the school. Once the position is filled, the need for the committee goes out of existence.

3. *Coordinating committees* are ones that provide general direction and guidance. An example would be the executive committee. This committee typically includes the officers of the board and may include committee chairs and perhaps other board members.

As stated earlier, committee functions should be clearly stated, and for standing committees, they should be defined in the school's bylaws. Minutes from board meetings should indicate when special committees are established.

In many cases board members have an opportunity to indicate their committee preferences when they come onto a board. The board chair usually appoints committee members and often, but not always, attempts to follow the wishes of the board member.

Such appointments typically are made with the input of the committee chair as well as the head of school. As provided in many bylaws, the chair and the head are ex officio members of each committee and serve without vote.

Committee appointment is one of the most important responsibilities of the chair. Competence, interest, expertise, skills, and, above all, understanding what is best for the school are key factors in making these appointments.

Committee Members Outside of the Board

It is not uncommon for many schools to have board committees that include both board and non-board members. These non-board committee members may provide specific knowledge or expertise in a particular area. Depending on the person's interest level, the board may decide to ask the non-board member to consider joining the board.

Non-board members who serve on board committees rarely serve as the committee's chair. There are certain exceptions to this practice, but they are not the norm. The board chair is almost always a current member of the board of trustees.

CASE STORY #12

Financial Assistance: What Information Is Appropriate to Share?

Emily had been the treasurer and chair of the finance committee for only a few months. She and her husband, Steven, had two boys at the school. During their time at the school they had been active, involved, and a pleasure to work with. When David, the head of school, suggested that Emily should be considered to be a trustee, he was completely confident that she would make an excellent member of the board. She had always demonstrated a great attitude, never appeared to have an agenda, never asked for special treatment from teachers, and had been a generous donor. All characteristics indicated that, with appropriate training, she could be an excellent trustee.

Following Emily's election to the board things began to change. David noticed that Emily showed signs of wanting special treatment for her children. For example, she began complaining that her son wasn't receiving enough playing time on the middle school basketball team even though he was an excellent basketball player. She expressed her displeasure at the school's admission of a few academically questionable students (in her opinion) who happened to be highly accomplished athletes. She didn't like that these new students were taking playing time away from her son, and she seemed to use her role as a new trustee to make her case. Needless to say, David was alarmed.

At the time of her appointment to the board, one of the factors in her favor was that she was a highly respected accountant and a partner in a large accounting firm. David was certain she would make an excellent treasurer and chair of the finance committee.

When the previous treasurer stepped down, Emily was the obvious choice.

Over the past several years the school's accounts receivable had become a challenge and an area the school was taking steps to correct under David's leadership. Apparently, however, not at the rate that Emily found acceptable. In addition, the economy was not helping, and some families were falling behind. The school had historically tried hard to work with families, though sometimes this backfired—thus the issue with accounts receivable. David and the board had been in agreement on how to move forward to correct the problem.

Enter Emily with a different agenda. Her goal was to institute a set of policies that restricted the school's ability to work with families to extend grace while they temporarily struggled to remain current. She insisted on knowing who was behind and demanded that policies be strictly enforced. Nothing was off limits, including suspension for being behind in payments all the way to expulsion. She was convicted that this was the most appropriate way to get on top of the challenge of accounts receivable. Of course, each school must set policies or guidelines that determine when it is necessary to ensure tuition payments are made. And certainly, there are situations that call for serious action to be taken. However, should members of the board have access to personal information about a family's financial situation? Can the argument be made that because the board has fiduciary responsibility for the school, they should be privy to such information?

Different schools approach the budgeting process differently. Often it is a joint process between the finance committee, the head of school, and the business manager. At some schools the head, business manager, and senior staff work out budget details and ultimately present the budget to the board for approval. The head will discuss different aspects of the budget and explain the rationale behind a range of recommendations—perhaps first to the finance committee and ultimately the full board. At most independent and faith-based schools, the budget becomes a recommendation of the finance committee (and the treasurer) to the entire board. David had a strong belief that while the board has fiduciary responsibility for the school, the board should not have line-item veto (control) but rather an overall understanding of how the budget works, including revenue generation and expense control. The budget for financial assistance is part of the overall strategy to ensure the school's financial future.

On the one hand David supported strategies to reduce accounts receivable. But on the other hand, he was convinced the current strategy of working closely with families and communicating with them to resolve their financial issues was the best approach. Perhaps what concerned David the most was what he considered to be Emily's heavy-handed approach and demand of the letter of the policy with no consideration for family circumstances. She even wanted to know the names of any family that was behind according to the new policy. And during all of this, the board allowed her to do whatever she thought was best with minimal concern for the long-term effects this policy would have on the culture of the school. Would enforcing her policy with no exceptions create an atmosphere of resentment or would she be hailed as the savior of the school?

Questions for Discussion

1. *Should the board and board chair allow one person with an agenda to insist that her way is the only way to correct the accounts receivable issue?*
2. *Should financial assistance and issues surrounding accounts receivable be viewed as an operational issues in which the head of school is ultimately responsible, or are they a board matter in which the board sets the policy and oversees its implementation?*
3. *Other treasurers had seen no need to step into this issue. What was the trigger for Emily?*
4. *What limits should be placed on the board with regard to obtaining a family's personal information?*

Chapter Twelve

◆

Boards and Fundraising: Financially Committing to the School's Future

Perhaps the task of an independent and faith-based school board that is most often misunderstood or neglected during the recruitment process is that of fundraising on behalf of the school. Often these issues reveal the need for better ongoing communication about expectations.

Understanding Fundraising Principles

A candid dialogue is needed so that there is no misunderstanding when the time comes for the board to give, both individually and collectively. If this expectation is not made clear don't be surprised when there is some resentment to the request. It is imperative that board members understand and embrace fundraising principles. Philanthropy has numerous facets and some of the basic ones include:

People Want to Make Gifts

People don't give because they are forced to make a gift. Reflect for a moment on your own giving patterns. There are often several motivating factors in your decision to make a contribution. Ultimately you give because you have a desire to, you care deeply about the organization and its mission, and because you want to make a difference.

People Give to Make a Change for Good

The organization must demonstrate *why* it is important for people to give. It must be explained that the gift can be responsible for the good the organization is doing. People won't give simply because you have been in existence for a long time. They won't give because of a compelling story or mission. Much more is necessary. In seeking gifts, your strategy should embrace that reality and motivation on the part of donors.

People Give to Opportunities, Not Needs

More often than not, people respond to a compelling vision, not to the organization's budgetary needs. People want to give because they have been presented with an opportunity to achieve something special and meaningful, not because the organization "needs the money." It is completely inadequate to say you need money. A compelling vision that demonstrates the impact of the organization—that is what will win the day.

People Give to Success, not Distress

Donors want to believe that their support is going to further the mission of a successful, thriving organization. Organizations that struggle with leadership, mission, or finances have a much more difficult time convincing prospective donors of their viability and whether or not they can achieve what they say they can.

The Board's Responsibility for Fundraising

Almost every description you will find of the board of trustees will include statements regarding fundraising. As a 501(c)(3) nonprofit organization, the board of trustees has a clearly defined fiduciary responsibility meaning that the financial health of the school falls within their responsibilities. As a result, some boards will no doubt see that part of the financial health revolves around contributing financial resources to ensure the school's health and sustainability.

It is practically a universal truth in fundraising that donors to a school will take their cue from the board as to how generous they will be, or whether they will give at all. The principle behind this statement directly addresses the issue that those closest to understanding and embracing the school's mission are most likely the ones providing significant support. It follows then that if these people don't support the school, why should anyone else? In other words, if you can't get the board to give, how are you going to convince anyone else to give? It is not only a fair question; it is *the* question that must be addressed before any other.

There are those boards that believe that fundraising can be delegated to the school's head and development/advancement staff (if the school has made this much-needed investment). While delegating certain functions is very appropriate, it should not be assumed that they are now somehow exempt from any further involvement in fundraising.

The question sometimes arises as to the necessity of establishing a foundation for the purpose of raising funds.

Many public universities, public libraries, and public schools, for example, have created foundations for the purpose of raising funds on behalf of the organizations they serve. These foundations may also have their own board. However, an independent or faith-based school has no legal reason to create such a foundation. In the event the school establishes a foundation and a board to oversee their activities, the governing board of the school should still maintain involvement and support for fundraising.

Positioning the Board to Be Successful

For the board of trustees to understand and embrace their responsibilities in giving and participating in the different aspects of the fundraising process, it is imperative that they be encouraged to participate in training and educational opportunities that will increase their knowledge and understanding of how they can make the greatest impact possible. This includes leadership from the head of school, the chief development officer, the development committee, and chair. Communicating the value of participating in such events elevates this issue to an entirely different level.

Ways to Help Without Asking for Money

How often has it been said, "I'll do anything *but* fundraising!" People will attempt all kinds of dangerous stunts, but ask them to solicit a gift and they break out in a sweat. Fundraising is much more than *asking* for a gift. There is a process, and board members have numerous opportunities to assist with this other than asking for a gift.

Contributing
This should be the first step for every board member. Every board member should contribute as generously as they are able—

recognizing that giving should be a priority during the time of service on the board. The board must be 100 percent in financial support before going to others to ask for support. When prospective board members are recruited, the expectation for giving to the school and making the school one of your top three giving priorities is a vital conversation to have with prospective members.

Formulating Plans, Programs, Mission, and Case

Each of these is vital to the effectiveness of the school and represents an important responsibility of the board. The plans, programs, mission, and case are individually and collectively supported by a viable and vibrant fundraising program. Board members on the development committee, or elsewhere on the board, must provide meaningful leadership to ensure that each of these activities is achieved.

Building the List of Prospective Donors

The school may rely heavily on the need to ever expand its base of support. A fundamental way this happens is that individuals who care deeply about the school are in an ideal position to identify alumni, other individuals, foundations, and corporations who have similar interests. Board members have a "sphere of influence" that can be accessed to gain support for the school. It is imperative that they be approached about how best to accomplish this.

Researching and Evaluating Prospects

Never underestimate the importance and value of research on prospects and the preparation needed before a major gift visit is made. Board members may be in a position to provide helpful information that impacts the amount and manner in which the prospective donor is approached. All too often there are false assumptions about the capacity and inclination of prospects. Take as much guesswork as possible out of the process to ensure the best possible result.

Cultivating Prospects

People are more likely to give when they have a relationship with individuals who are in some way connected to the school. It is hard to beat the personal touch. Cultivating prospects by providing information and insight about the mission and vision of the school can be a very successful strategy in bringing forward more donors.

Making Introductions

By making the most of connections board members have, they can introduce others to those they do not feel comfortable soliciting. Smoothing the way for someone else to solicit can go far in securing that gift. Networking is a vital piece of the fundraising picture. Board members have great connections, and these connections should be put to work on behalf of the school.

Helping and Supporting Fundraising Events

Events are a time-consuming enterprise for even the best of schools. Under certain circumstances the focus shifts from the goal of raising funds for the school to other factors such as the social aspects of the event. Focus on the fundraising should not be lost in the dialogue. Board members can play an essential role supporting these events by serving on the committee(s) charged with holding the event. Depending on the complexity and ambition of the event, there may well be numerous ways for board members to be supportive.

Getting Out Annual Fund Appeal Letters

Sending out annual fund appeal letters is one of those traditions that still linger in this age of online communication. If your school sends out these letters, why not add something special to the appeal—a note from the board chair or another member of the board? It is an appropriate way to stay connected to prospective or existing donors without stepping over the line into operational matters. It's all about connecting to the school's numerous constituencies including parents, alumni, parents of alumni, grandparents, and others.

Writing Thank-You Notes

Even in an age of texting and e-mails, nothing trumps a handwritten note of thanks for someone's generosity. This is genuine stewardship—taking the time to say thank you in a way rarely seen today. Board members can support this effort—especially when the member has been involved with identifying the donor and/or soliciting the gift.

Motivating and Inspiring Others

Motivation, inspiration, encouragement, support, and communication all play a significant role in leadership. It is important that board members motivate one another and hold one another accountable for the success of the school. What is it that will motivate a board member to become more engaged? A general appeal at a board meeting is not nearly as effective as a direct, personal appeal from the board chair. Think about that when you are considering how to get someone to do something that needs to be done.

One of the biggest challenges in working with and motivating board members is to get them to do *what* they say they will do, *when* they say they will do it! Board members are volunteers—but volunteers who have a commitment. Successful and inspired boards have this challenge figured out.

In the end, there are four primary areas where board members struggle with fundraising:

1. Board members often do not understand philanthropic giving and asking. They fail to recognize that people want to give and take great joy in doing so.

2. Board members are reluctant to accept the fact that part of what comes with being on a board is fundraising. Rare is the independent or faith-based school that does not have a need to raise funds and rare is the board that escapes this responsibility.

3. Board members do not grasp the concept that there are many ways to be involved in the fundraising process without directly soliciting a gift. There is magic in the process and often board members can assist in securing the gift without asking for the gift.

4. Board members are slow to realize the most effective way to motivate and encourage members to act is to personally ask that they accept specific assignments—including the encouragement to support fundraising efforts.

Chapter Thirteen

◆

The Board's Role in Planned Giving

Planned giving, sometimes referred to as deferred giving, is a fundraising path that some schools traverse with great confidence. Often schools that have been in operation for a long time have developed planned giving programs yielding impressive results. For schools that are younger, the focus is more on current, recurring giving such as the annual fund. Planned giving for schools tends to focus more on the establishment of bequests and encouraging alumni to consider putting the school in estate planning.

Whether planned giving or current giving, the board of trustees must be "all in" supporting the program by their own giving and by working with the development staff to create the best possible program. If the school develops such a program, with the support and endorsement of the board, it often follows that an ad hoc committee consisting of board members, major donors, and development staff from the school come together to form a planned giving committee.

Seven Fundraising Truisms

It is in this committee's best interest to adopt a list of fundraising truisms designed to set the tone for the rationale for giving to the school and for committing to a program of encouraging planned gifts be made to the school.

Fundraising Truism 1: People will give because they choose to do so. Generous donors take great joy in giving and pride in supporting an institution that is meeting needs and preparing leaders for a more complex world than they inherited.

Fundraising Truism 2: People want to give to independent schools because such schools have in their DNA a desire to change the world for the better, recognizing that the educational experience being provided is building those traits that will serve our society and our culture well.

Fundraising Truism 3: People give when the request is made by a peer, or friend, or colleague who is respected and when there is shared vision. A personal request coupled with a discussion of what is involved has the potential to have an enormous impact on the person being asked. The better the donor is known, the more likely he or she is willing to make a contribution to the school.

Fundraising Truism 4: People give not so much because you have needs but rather because there is a definite recognition that the school meets needs. Independent and faith-based schools are in a strong position to provide a values-laden education that reveals leadership of every kind. Whether leadership in business, nonprofit organizations, churches and faith-based ministries, or organizations of any type, independent schools give the unmistakable impression of providing the education that will produce individuals passionate about making a positive impact on the world. As a result, these schools will enjoy support from their constituencies.

Fundraising Truism 5: People find it more compelling to support a thriving school that has a track record of success and a strategic direction that outlines a vision worthy of consideration. Schools that are struggling with enrollment, programmatic issues, or a poor campus environment have a much more difficult and challenging time raising funds. Often this perception leads prospective donors to believe they might be supporting a school with questionable viability. This is not the environment that schools will find conducive to raising support for whatever the school is seeking to fund.

Fundraising Truism 6: People choose to make a planned gift because they want to leave a lasting legacy. Gifts are made for a variety of motives but near the top of the list is that the donor wants to make a difference and do so in a way that the contribution, often as an endowed gift, is in perpetuity.

Fundraising Truism 7: With the occasional exception, generally speaking, you don't get what you don't ask for. Gifts, including planned gifts, are made as the result of a strategic effort to match up the donor's wishes with the school's needs and priorities. There is genuine magic when this happens in such a way that benefits both the donor and the school.

Making Sure the Planned Giving Program Makes a Difference

To ensure that the board understands the place of the planned giving program in the context of the school's overall development program, the following questions must be raised:

1. *What is the attitude of the board chair toward the planned giving program?* Support for the program must come from the chair of the board with him or her leading by example in making a planned gift.

2. *What expectations has the board set regarding planned giving?* It is important for the board to take the lead from the school's development leadership team. One of the most impactful messages the board chair, the head of school, and the development director can share is the necessity for every board member to participate in the planned giving program.

3. *How can a board retreat instill a spirit and a culture of collaboration?* The board retreat may be the ideal opportunity for the board, head of school, and development leadership to come together and recognize the obligation every trustee has to make a planned giving program a priority—and a long-term priority at that. An ongoing endeavor will yield results over time while having limited effect in the short-term.

From an organizational perspective, the school must take the steps required for the planned giving program to make a difference. Typically, this means the introduction of a *planned giving committee* that includes trustees—members of the development committee, head of school, development director, and individuals with expertise in this area (attorney, trust officer, etc.). The creation of a board committee on planned giving will make clear the board's seriousness on this issue.

One of the most important responsibilities of the planned giving committee is the creation of the manner and means by which generosity to the school through a planned gift will be recognized. This new donor recognition "society" must bear the name of some unique characteristic of the school. It would be easy to call this group the Legacy Society. However, that is much too generic and does not provide the prospective donor with the opportunity to have a unique connection with his or her school. Consider the following as they pertain to your school as a possibility for the name of the planned giving group:

- The year the school was founded
- The name of the founder or first head of school
- The name of the first board chair
- A unique tradition that the school is known for
- The location of the school
- A major benefactor
- The school's motto

Creating a name that is unique to the school will help connect the donor to the school in subtle but profound ways.

If the strategic importance of planned giving is not carefully thought through, there could be the tendency for the program to be overshadowed by the school's need to secure current gifts. Annual giving will always be viewed as critical because this program directly impacts the budget of the school. Only in rare circumstances is the annual fund outside of the budgetary process. Therefore, it must become a priority for the development office and for the board. Once again, the fundraising rule of thumb must be communicated to the board of trustees: *We cannot expect others to give until we as board are 100 percent in support of the initiative.*

Every trustee must ask themselves two fundamental questions: 1) Can I make the planned giving program a personal philanthropic priority for me? 2) Do I have the school as one of my top three organizations that I financially support? An affirmative answer to both will go a long way in helping the program meet its objectives.

What follows is that each individual trustee must ask, what can I do to support the program? The following are examples of putting these priorities in practice:

- Each trustee must set the tone by making a financial commitment to the planned giving program.
- Each trustee must suggest and participate in a process that identifies prospective donors.
- Each trustee must participate in soliciting gift commitments either by asking or making the introductions for others to ask for the support.
- Each trustee must express gratitude for the generosity for planned gift commitments. Creatively thanking donors is excellent stewardship and positions the school for the next ask.

The reality is that each trustee will not participate in all of the above. It should, however, be the standard by which every trustee is strongly encouraged to be engaged to the greatest extent possible.

Planned giving may not be for every independent or faith-based school, or a viable option given a school's current circumstances. But as the school matures, has more donors and more alumni, then the conversation should begin to take place. A comprehensive fundraising program for the school, in the long run, is going to include a planned giving program. This is the reality that every head of school who currently does not have a program will have to face. The good news is that your colleagues stand ready to assist and the opportunities to learn from your peers, as well as through professional development, are numerous and especially beneficial to schools with limited resources and development staff.

Chapter Fourteen

◆

Appropriate and Meaningful Support: The Board's Role in the Enrollment Management Process

K ey questions often arise as a board strives to ensure supporting the enrollment management process, yet the answers are a mix of confusion and misinformation that give rise to uncertainty and sometimes inaction, leaving the board without a direction to move forward. Preparing ahead of time as to how you will answer such important questions should bring clarity and provide a plan of action so the board can effectively partner with the school and be supportive but not intrusive in the school's admissions process. Consider the role and relationship of the board in the enrollment management effort and process of an independent school or faith-based school.

What is the board's role and responsibility in the school's enrollment management process?

The governing board of an independent or faith-based school is the channel through which passes not only governing and fiduciary responsibilities but also responsibilities for ensuring the school's success. The board must be supportive and encouraging of the marketing, communications, and development functions—all of which play a pivotal role in the success of enrollment management. Board members should never engage in actual admission decisions but they can effectively serve as ambassadors for the school who promote and advocate for the school. This ambassador role is key and should be discussed as part of board orientation.

How effective is the board in fulfilling these responsibilities, and what steps can be taken to improve trustee performance?

Just as it is with other responsibilities, some boards are more effective than others. It really comes back to setting expectations with prospective board members. Is it explained that a part of the board's culture is finding appropriate ways to participate in supporting the school's admissions and marketing efforts? Each board member should be provided a list of three to five ways he or she can support and engage in the enrollment management process. The board chair and head of school should set the tone by articulating ways to engage the board.

How should the head of school be involved in working with the board in supporting enrollment management?

The head must recognize that the board can be a strategic partner in enrollment. The board's chair, along with the head, should communicate with both individual trustees as well as the collective board to discover ways in which they can help. The board of trustees should defer to the head's wishes when it comes to specifics. This should be made clear during the board recruitment and onboarding process. The board chair and the head should discover ways to ensure that this issue stays in front of the entire board.

Do you see any conflicts with the board being involved in the enrollment management process and influencing admissions decisions?

There are certainly possibilities for conflicts to arise. For example, the board should not be involved in making decisions regarding which students are admitted and which are not. Parents must be assured that their children are admitted on the merits of the application they submit—grades, activities, character, etc. Certainly, a trustee may express his or her support for a candidate. However, favoritism is all too frequently a concern for parents, and once it is known that a trustee is influencing the admissions process, a level of trust is lost that is often difficult to recover. There are appropriate roles for the board, but attempting to manipulate and dictate admissions decisions is not one of them.

What is the most effective way a board chair can support and encourage the head and enrollment team while recognizing the staff works for/with the head not the chair?

While the board has a fiduciary responsibility, and is the school's governing body, they can still be part of the team that supports such activities as admissions. The board chair, in particular should find ways he or she can be supportive and not intrusive.

Here are a few ideas:

- Demonstrate support by providing a message on the school's website indicating gratitude for people's interest in the school by visiting the website. Such a message from the board chair can go with the head's message.
- Be visible and speak at the school's open house or other admissions events. The message from the chair is a simple but profound one—the head and admissions professionals have the full support of the board of trustees.
- Include the director of enrollment management by providing him or her an opportunity to give a report at each board meeting or ask this leader to be on the admissions or marketing committee if the board has such a committee.

What are your thoughts about having a standing committee of the board for enrollment management?

A standing committee for admissions/enrollment management can be both positive and negative. On the positive side, having such a committee raises the level of awareness for the whole admissions process. Having a better understanding of all that goes into student recruitment and retention will cause board members to be more understanding and supportive of the process. The standing committee's ability to communicate this to the full board only creates a new level of attentiveness to a central issue for the school.

On the negative side, you don't want this committee to start dictating what kind of cookies to serve at an open house or whatever admissions event you are having. You also don't want such a committee involved in the process of deciding who is admitted and who is not. A standing committee can be effective—just make certain it is focusing on process and on building an awareness of the challenges and opportunities that will have the greatest impact.

What is the most effective way to engage and communicate with the board regarding enrollment management?

The most effective way to communicate with the board is for the head of school or possibly the director of admissions (director of enrollment management) to report at each board meeting. If the school has a board committee, it stands to reason that the admissions director would be the liaison to the board and therefore attend board meetings. The case can be made that this staff leader should attend board meetings because of the central role that enrollment management plays as the primary revenue generator of the school. The head of school is in a position to report on enrollment strategy, but the admissions director is in a key position to answer questions concerning process with up-to-date data.

What do enrollment management professionals need to know about the school's board of trustees?

The board makes a range of decisions that impact the school with regard to policy and strategy that may impact the admissions/enrollment management process. Having a general understanding of the board's work including the bylaws would be helpful. Also, it would be very important for the admissions team to understand the kind of decisions the board makes. Of course, the board sets tuition that directly affects the budget. Also, the amount of financial or tuition assistance and issues such as diversity influence tuition and financial assistance decisions. The board should also be aware of how net tuition revenue impacts enrollment. However, the board typically looks to the head of school and the enrollment management director for guidance on setting tuition and tuition assistance policies. The admissions professionals must work with the head of school and have an ongoing dialogue about understanding how the board can be advocates for the admissions team and admissions process.

* * *

This is an area in which the board can, as individual board members, maximize their sphere of influence to encourage prospective families to consider the school as the best choice for their children. When, at board meetings, the chair and head of school make an appeal for trustees to assist with some aspect of the admissions process, board members should be prepared to provide the support that is requested. At the same time, the board chair and the head of school can and should encourage all board members to determine how to best advocate for growing the school.

CASE STORY #13
Authority of the Interim Head

The relationship between the head of school, the board chair, and a member of the senior administrative team is an interesting one and one with the potential for miscommunication that leads to unfortunate consequences. Best practices would suggest that the board chair and the administrative officer would have fairly limited contact and that some, if not much, of that contact would be filtered through the head of school. This is considered to be a best practice because the board (and the board chair) has one employee—the head of school. What happens when this best practice breaks down? The consequences can be devastating!

David arrived at the school bright and early one Monday morning in July. Just a few weeks earlier he had been appointed as the interim head of school at Brookside School. Brookside is a pre-K through sixth grade school of approximately three hundred students. The school had the understandable practice of the curriculum director working closely with the division heads. The previous head had retired, and the board appointed David to the post of interim head. This was the second time he had served in an interim role and based on conversations with the board, he was excited by this opportunity.

David felt that his first task was to get to know the administrative team and listen to their thoughts regarding concerns, challenges, as well as opportunities. He felt it was his task to listen and learn and then act when he thought it was appropriate to do so. Introductions were made, words of welcome were extended, and David opened the meeting with prayer. He then went around the room of nine administrative team leaders and listened, occasionally interjecting a thought, comment, or question. After approximately two hours the meeting came to a close and David thanked everyone for their positive attitude and support during this important leadership transition.

Soon after David's arrival as the interim head position Scott, the director of curriculum, asked to meet with him. David had already been warned that there were issues with Scott. Many with whom he had spoken talked of numerous trust concerns as well as other issues regarding confidentiality and understanding of fundamental questions having to do with best practices in the curriculum development process. While Scott no doubt brought certain skills and qualities to the position, his deficiencies were a concern. David believed he could work with him, but it was going to be a challenge.

The meeting began with Scott professing his support and belief that hiring David was a very positive move for the school. After a few minutes of basic pleasantries, he abruptly announced his intention to go to the board chair over an issue involving the lower school head. David was stunned and understandably asked why. Scott claimed he had been considering this for some time when the previous head retired under what he described as "unusual circumstances," and Scott questioned David's authority as the interim. He went on to indicate that he had philosophical differences with the direction of the lower school and directly questioned the leadership of the lower school head. They talked for a while, and David made it clear that approaching the board regarding any personnel matter was inappropriate. He tried to discern whether or not Scott understood the issue that the board has only one employee—the head of school. Finally, David asked him to think about it over the weekend and said that they would talk about this again on Monday.

On several levels David thought Scott's timing was inappropriate. He knew that if Scott persisted on this path he would have no choice but to terminate him for insubordination. David recognized all of the new school year activities that related to the curriculum and academic program would begin in just a few weeks. It would be difficult to have someone step in. Plus, he knew that Scott had influence in the school community and was friendly with several of the board members. David's first thought was to contact the board chair.

On Friday, David met with Dan, the board chair, to discuss the situation. David shared with Dan a detailed summary of the conversation he and Scott had earlier in the day. Dan was surprised and concerned that Scott did not understand the hierarchy of the school. He clearly thought the school would be fine if Scott had to leave, but hoped he would realize the magnitude of the mistake he was making. In David's mind this was an internal personnel matter that for the most part was not the purview of the board. He grasped the uniqueness of the circumstances, which was why he contacted Dan. Otherwise he felt no particular obligation to communicate a personnel matter with the chair. However, he knew surprises like this were not welcomed by the trustees. As far as he was concerned it was Dan's decision whether or not to inform the board.

Monday morning rolled around and David met with Scott to discuss the situation. It was apparent that Scott was conflicted and having second thoughts about what he was considering. He agreed, for the time being, that he would not contact the board chair. David was very relieved and expressed his appreciation for Scott's understanding the gravity of the situation.

Over the next two weeks, David had the impression that things were going well, and he and Scott communicated occasionally over a range of academic and curricular activities. But then Scott came to David and said he had been thinking about his future. He stated he was thinking again about approaching the board chair, but that he would refrain for now. David met from time to time with Dan (board chair) to keep him in the loop regarding the unfolding drama. He was completely unprepared for the events that were about to unfold.

David's last conversation with Scott had been on Thursday in which he confirmed his decision to not communicate with Dan his concerns with the lower school head. But that all changed on Sunday evening when David received an e-mail from Scott indicating he would meet with the chair Monday morning. He stated in his e-mail message that he simply could not work with the lower school head and was terribly disappointed that David had not been more proactive in addressing Scott's concern about this person.

On Monday morning David once again met with Scott. David couldn't remember ever working with someone who was simply unconcerned with the consequences of his actions. He could not recall ever working with someone who was unprofessional and unable to comprehend how an independent or faith-based school operates. While David was no psychologist, this seemed like classic passive-aggressive behavior. This time it appeared that Scott's decision was final. He was going to communicate with the chair. David had no choice but to terminate Scott effective immediately. David then drafted a statement announcing Scott's termination. He sought input from the director of communications and together they completed the final version of the announcement. The plan was to e-mail the announcement to the school's parents following an afternoon meeting with the faculty and staff.

David also communicated to the board chair about Scott's termination including the prepared announcement. David encouraged Dan and board members to direct any questions they had received to him. Later that day Dan sent the announcement to the board. One board member, Frank, was very upset! He was furious that the board had not been informed that Scott was considering such a move. Frank, without consulting the board chair, called David about the matter. What ensued was a very difficult and unpleasant conversation. Frank accused David of mismanaging the situation, telling him that he had been on the job for thirty days and therefore was not in a position to withhold this kind of information from the board. David calmly reminded Frank of two fundamental issues. First, he had in fact informed and continued to inform the board chair of the events taking place. As far as David was concerned, it was Dan's decision whether or not to inform the entire board. Second, and critical to this discussion, David reminded Frank that the board had one employee and that *all* personnel decisions were, in the final analysis, made by the head. David made it clear that in addition to informing the board chair, he had done everything possible to work with Scott to convince him not to go directly to the board with his concerns.

Frank stated this was a special circumstance that superceded any policy and that David should have informed the board directly, and at the time of Scott's first discussion with him. David asked him, where do you start and stop with "special circumstances" situations and board interference with personnel issues? David was adamant and tried to make it clear to Frank that the board either has one employee or it doesn't. As the bitter conversation was winding down, Frank stated that he planned to have a thorough discussion of this matter with the board at its upcoming board meeting. David said they would have to agree to disagree and hoped there could be some kind of reconciliation to the matter.

Following the conversation David contacted Dan to make sure he was aware of Frank's intention to make this an issue that would be discussed at the next board meeting. David was faced with a difficult situation and one that might compromise his principles as the head of school. As he reflected on the bizarre dynamics that had brought the school to this point, he thought the actions of a few could result in the school's board making one of the unhealthiest decisions he had ever encountered. Would he survive the board meeting? He was convinced that his chances of doing so were limited. He had done what he thought was right. If the board thought otherwise, there wasn't much he could do. Although he reflected on all that had taken place, he was confident he had done what was in the best interest of the school. What would happen next was beyond his control.

Prior to the next board meeting, board chair Dan took the opportunity to communicate to each board member, taking responsibility for not contacting the board about the ongoing situation with Scott. Having done this, he hoped the conversation with the board would be limited. Unfortunately, this was not to be the case. Frank began this discussion by insisting that the board be informed of any member of the faculty and staff who is considering directly contacting the board chair regarding a personnel matter rather going through proper personnel channels. Although David was philosophically opposed to this. Was the board acting in this matter because he was the interim? He reminded the board that this was, in fact, the action he had taken, that is, to inform Dan, the board chair. He was not seeking Dan's approval but to let him know what had taken place. Still, he was prepared to resign if the board reinstated Scott. He indicated that he would communicate with Dan, and that Dan would communicate with the other board members. David was understandably concerned that a dangerous precedent had been set. Fortunately, the board did reaffirm their commitment to stay out of personnel issues once a head of school was in place. All David could do was hope this would be the case. Only time and circumstances would determine how the board reacts the next time a similar personnel matter captured their attention. During the remainder of his term as interim, no other personnel changes took place at the school.

Questions for Discussion

1. *What is the ideal relationship between the head of school and board chair?*
2. *What role should an individual trustee play in making statements and demands on the head?*
3. *What is the appropriate way for an individual member of the board to communicate with the head of school?*
4. *What role should the board play in personnel matters?*
5. *In personnel matters, should there be a difference between an interim head and a permanent one?*

Chapter Fifteen

◆

The Connection Between Supportive Boards and Successful Schools

Growth is not the only metric independent schools consider when evaluating their health. However, many schools measure part of their success and sustainability based on how well they are attracting new students and retaining those currently enrolled. There are numerous reasons and definite strategies from an enrollment management and marketing perspective that will impact growth. Often overlooked in this discussion is the health of the governing board and how the board relates and interacts with the head of school.

When a school grows approximately 25 percent from the previous year, there must be identifiable ways in which the school can review the strategies that contributed to the success and assess what factors were involved in such growth. While there are indeed numerous reasons for enrollment growth, much of the credit for the substantial increase is directly attributable to having an exceptionally healthy governing board.

The governing board is not typically recognized or credited as a reason for school growth. But if reflecting on a few of the more important responsibilities of the board, then the correlation becomes apparent. Without question, first among the most valued roles of the board is working together as a team, and second is supporting the head of school. The meaningful acceptance and understanding of these two huge factors cannot be overestimated. And yet schools often fail to see the warning signs of discord, poor performance, lack of knowledge regarding best practices, and failure to adequately support the head leading them toward a number of negative consequences including no growth or even declining enrollment.

While acknowledging the correlation and connection between a board's health and issues such as school growth, why do we find examples of schools thriving under the direction of boards that are unhealthy, perhaps even dysfunctional? Any such example is the exception and not the norm. The answer for this unusual circumstance can likely be found in exceptional administrative leadership. This can be the case if the head of school is a strong leader and the leadership group that he or she works with function as a team with a high level of effectiveness and efficiency. It could be argued that the absence of support, encouragement, collaboration, and trust coming from the board forces the school's leadership to more clearly focus on what needs to be done to ensure the health of the school. To be sure, it is a challenge for the school's head and other leaders, but if the right leadership team is in place, they can often overcome a weak, ineffective board.

Governing boards that desire to adhere to best practices are in the stronger position to realize that there is a connection between effective board leadership, effective school leadership, and the health of both the board and the school. To begin with, boards have three very specific and fundamental responsibilities:

1. It is mandatory that the board develops and approves the mission of the school. While they may seek input regarding wording, phraseology, or intent, in the end the board accepts responsibility for what is stated in the mission statement that gives purpose and direction to the school.
2. The board must accept fiduciary responsibility for the school. It is their role to ensure that the school is financially sustainable. This includes approval of the budget as well as advancing the strategy for long-term growth. The function of tuition, annual giving, capital giving, endowment, and all forms of revenue generation ultimately lands at the door of the governing board.
3. The board hires the head of school and board members support that individual to the best of their ability. While occasionally it is inevitable that a change in leadership must take place, the board should consider replacing the head only after an extensive process of evaluation has been considered. The belief of hiring and firing as a concept should be replaced with hiring and supporting. Every head of school understands their reporting relationship with the board. But if the head believes that the board is supportive and working together for what is in the best interest of the school, then he or she can lead with confidence, knowing the board is there to provide valuable support.

In addition to these fundamental responsibilities, there are specific responsibilities that have to do with familiarity of school programs and marketing initiatives as well as awareness and advocacy for those programs. Board members should embrace their ambassador roles and the board chair should be the primary cheerleader for ensuring this occurs. Each board member has a sphere of influence and should use that influence to build awareness in the community among those who might not be acquainted with the school or certain specific aspects of the school. It is significantly important that the chair articulate the magnitude of this responsibility and provide precise examples of how this works. The head of school can support this initiative as well. The head can provide information, material, and accompany the board member to foster these connections and build greater appreciation for the school.

When thinking about what determines the board's health several factors must be considered, of which foremost would have to be the board selection process. Is there a committee on trustees (or a governance committee), and is that committee charged with recruitment, orientation, education, and evaluation of board members? This is a thorough process that stipulates the school will make every effort to secure the services and support of trustees who truly understand and embrace their roles and responsibilities. The result is a stronger, healthier board and a stronger, healthier school.

In an effort to ensure that the board is as strong as possible, the recruitment process must include a discussion of expectations. Are board members expected to attend meetings? Are they expected to serve on a committee? Are they expected to give as generously as they are capable? Are they expected to recognize the difference between their role and the head's? Such issues must be addressed to bring additional clarity to the role of a board member. All independent and faith-based schools want engaged and contributing board members. By illuminating expectations, board members are better prepared to serve with distinction.

What should naturally follow an excellent recruitment process and communication of expectations is a belief that board education and board culture make a difference. Does the board want to be a best-practices board that includes a method for some type of board education? Does the board conduct retreats annually or at least periodically? Does the board retain individuals who have expertise and experience in working with governing boards of independent or faith-based schools? These are the questions and the issues that will help determine the level of health and how it truly impacts the school in meaningful and productive ways.

Independent and faith-based schools face a range of challenges to achieving their mission. However, the work done at these schools in preparing students for a future that our culture desperately needs simply means that the stakes are enormous. And the ultimate responsibility for getting it right falls to the governing board. It is imperative that boards recognize the certain correlation between being a healthy board, adhering to best practices, and acknowledging that they can and should have a positive impact on school growth. This will have enormous positive consequences on the school's future.

Learning from the experience of schools that are experiencing substantial growth is a valuable lesson in acknowledging the principle that having a healthy board and a healthy school isn't merely something that sounds good but rather an expression and recognition of the reality that a school can best achieve its mission when there is a connection between the two.

CASE STORY #14

When the Board Chair Decides to Communicate with the School's Staff

Although Jefferson Academy was an established school, it's recent troubled history had included six heads of school in the last fifteen years. Independent school leaders know that this metric, more often than not, is a significant indicator of problems with the board of trustees and the head of school. Such was the case at Jefferson. Karen had been the board chair for two years and prior to that a trustee for a number of years. Also, there were no term limits which was another significant concern and one that should be a red flag to any prospective head of school. Chris had been head for less than a year and was already seeing signs of trouble with Karen. While he thought their relationship was okay, he was not prepared for what would come next.

One of Chris's biggest concerns was that Karen was not very familiar with best practices and/or the boundaries that should define the relationship between the board chair and head of school. She believed it was appropriate for her to do whatever she decided to do. Board roles of establishing the mission statement, generating the strategic plan, and supporting the head of school were mostly lost on her. She was not about to allow anyone to tell her what she could and could not do.

It was clear that Karen offered almost no trust, support, or encouragement to Chris. Instead she began an intentional campaign to undermine his authority with what appeared to be a concerted effort leading to his removal. Her latest tactic was to meet with staff in order to gain information that would be damaging to Chis and his ability to lead the school. When a staff member who had met with Karen came to him with the news of what was happening, Chris immediately insisted that Karen and he meet. She admitted she was meeting with a few of the staff with the explanation that it was the only method she could use to get information on what he was doing.

Chris was pretty confident this was someone he would have a difficult time working with to advance the school and its mission. The stakes were high—the school and his career were in serious jeopardy. Was there a way to explain to her that he was the only employee of the board and that she had no business making direct contact with a member of the staff regarding a board or governance issue? Karen was one of those individuals who believed that because she was the chair of the board, there was no one at Jefferson Academy that did not report to her.

In spite of his best efforts, there was nothing he could do to stop her from meeting with the staff whenever and wherever she chose. Sadly, it was time to move on. He knew the fundamental truism in every independent and faith-based school: *When there is trouble between the chair and the head, it is always the head who must depart.* He submitted his resignation and began making plans to move on.

As a trustee, the board chair has nothing, from a governance perspective, to communicate with individual members of the school's administrative staff. In addition, what would be the result if the board chair sought out members of the staff to discover any issues or concerns about the head of school? Such a scenario would raise three critical issues:

1. The chair should never go to a staff member to find out anything regarding the head.
2. As an individual, the board chair has no authority when communicating with staff.

3. Such behavior demonstrates a complete lack of support and trust for the head.

Questions for Discussion

1. *What can the head of school do should the board chair take matters into his or her hands as described above?*
2. *What factors usually lead to this type of behavior?*
3. *How would anyone on the faculty and staff feel were they approached by the board chair?*
4. *What does a scenario like the one above say about the culture of the board?*
5. *Why did Karen, the board chair, believe she had the authority to communicate with faculty and staff regarding such matters?*

Chapter Sixteen

◆

Executive Sessions: Out of Step with Best Practices

An independent school leader shared the disturbing and unfortunate news that the board of trustees had decided to start holding executive sessions. Such sessions are usually held after the conclusion of business from the regular board meeting. Excluded from the session are any staff who had attended the board meeting and ex-officio members of the board—including the head of school. These sessions come with a minefield of problems and issues for the school. In almost every circumstance executive sessions are destructive and inevitably lead to an atmosphere of distrust. They are a distraction and may lead to the departure of the head of school.

Why would the board decide to do this especially given that the head was very successful and the board had never had any reason to hold an executive session before? A new board chair had just begun his duties and wanted to include executive sessions. Then the next question must be, was the new chair sharing information discussed during the sessions with the head? The answer was no.

Information was being withheld for no apparent reason other than for the chair to demonstrate his power and authority over the head of school.

Why are executive sessions not healthy for schools and why is it that some board chairs have difficulty with this issue? Boards of independent and faith-based schools are unique but not that unique among nonprofit organizations. Here are the top five reasons why executive sessions are destructive to the school.

1. Executive sessions create a climate of mistrust between the head and the governing board.

One of the most important characteristics that must be present for school effectiveness is for the board chair and the head to trust one another, to respect and support the role that each must play. Executive sessions do not produce trust, respect, or support. Relationships built on these ideals invariably lead to stronger ties to the school and one another. This surely is more important and valuable than anything that would result from an executive session.

2. Executive sessions demonstrate that a true partnership is absent from the relationship.

Working together means just that. The head and board chair have different responsibilities and different perspectives, but they must work together to achieve mission and vision for the organization. Such sessions strongly suggest that they are not truly working together or creating a culture that will lead to a best-practices board.

3. Executive sessions may suggest the board has something to hide.

If they do not have something to hide, why hold these sessions? What is it that the board can't share with the head? Other than issues of evaluation and compensation there is no reason to keep anything from the head of school.

4. Executive sessions demonstrate a lack of understanding of the board's role.

All too often executive sessions are forums to spread gossip and discuss staff or other matters in unproductive and inappropriate ways. In no way should it ever be okay for the board to get the impression that this behavior is acceptable.

5. Executive sessions often include discussions about issues with which the board has limited or no information.

Meeting in the absence of the head, the board may lack the information needed to effectively discuss the matter. There are numerous circumstances in which the head has confidential information or information known only by a few people. Without his or her input, the discussion may result in an incorrect or unfortunate strategy.

There will be those who believe differently. They will argue that executive sessions are harmless and that thinking otherwise is simply paranoia. Some claim executive sessions are fine and should be a part of every meeting agenda. Independent school best practices would respectfully disagree. Does the board have a right and responsibility to discuss the performance of the head of school? Absolutely! How this is accomplished is the key. Does the board have the right to discuss other issues in the absence of the head (often an ex-officio member of the board)? Not if they wish to have a collaborative, trusting relationship with the head.

Is it possible that something constructive can result from these sessions? Yes, it is possible. But why exclude the head when this individual can add to any conversation the board is having regarding any issue? Schools and their boards should strive for more, to be better than this. They should be seeking to be the best possible school. Leadership is recognized in people of courage—individuals who inspire, motivate, support, and encourage. These are the kind of board members who will not make the mistake of equating executive sessions with doing the real work of the school. This is the kind of school that should be lifted up as an example of what best-practices governance looks like.

CASE STORY #15
The Importance of Trust Between the Head and Chair

There it was—on the table almost as soon as the words came out of Jeff's mouth. Jeff was facilitating a retreat for the board. He was discussing the most important responsibilities of the board and he was describing the incredibly important truism that the best, most successful independent schools are those in which the relationship between the head, the board chair, and entire governing body must be based on trust and support. The facts were these: twenty-one members on the board met five times a year with seven standing committees.

The retreat was focused on best practices for governance and the commencement of a strategic planning process that was to include a comprehensive assessment of all aspects of the school—including governance responsibilities. Jeff was in the process of sharing board responsibilities. Specifically, he was addressing the issue of the critical nature of the relationship between the head and board chair, the fact that this partnership set the tone for so much of what could be accomplished.

Jeff believed one of the very best examples for communicating this partnership was to state with candor and clarity why holding executive sessions—discussions by the board without the presence of the head—was a very bad idea and how such sessions resulted in distrust, suspicion, and a failure to provide support for the head. It was at this moment that the new chair of the board spoke up and expressed his opinion on this topic. "I see nothing wrong with having executive sessions. As long as the head and I have a relationship based on trust then I fail to see the harm in having an occasional executive session."

In Jeff's earlier comments he described the circumstances when having an executive session was appropriate, indeed necessary. This, he said, would be needed when the head was being evaluated and when their compensation package was being considered. Other than that, Jeff made it clear there really was no other reason to exclude the head. You were either partners or not. Following the board chair's comment, Jeff responded, "If your relationship is based on trust, then why do you not trust the head enough to include her in any conversation with the board?" The chair countered, "She knows that I support her in every way." Jeff responded, "What's support got to do with it? If you don't demonstrate trust then support seems to be just conversation without conviction."

The board chair paused a moment and admitted that perhaps he would need to reflect on this and rethink his position on executive sessions. Jeff thought this was a positive step on the board's understanding that they had a wide range of strategic challenges to address, but having executive sessions could be eliminated from the list.

Questions for Discussion

1. *What does this story tell you about the new board chair understanding his responsibilities?*
2. *Why is trust critical to the relationship between head and board chair?*
3. *Under what circumstances would this relationship be tested?*
4. *Support is such an important character trait the board chair must demonstrate at every opportunity. Reflecting on your own circumstances, can you cite examples of situations in which the board chair supported or backed you up when a difficult or controversial issue surfaced?*

Chapter Seventeen

◆

Board Evaluation: Key Components to Sustaining Excellence

A board's ability to meaningfully evaluate their work and impact on the school is erratic. Some boards do it well; other boards see little or no value in the process. The most useful way for sustaining excellence is to identify the key areas of self-evaluation and create the framework to provide the data and information necessary.

The different categories suggest those areas of work on which the board should be focused. Viewed as a questionnaire, these seven categories and questions should be answered with a "yes, we are doing this" or "no, we're not doing this." If the answer is "no," then the school must assign responsibility to ensure that the question can eventually be answered "yes." You'll find these questions listed again in Appendix H with space for your responses.

These key areas include:

- Planning
- Selection and composition
- Organization/structure
- Orientation and training
- Meetings
- Individual trustees (experienced and new)
- Head of school

Planning

The board should, almost above any other factor, be a group that devotes significant time to planning. The central questions in this area should include:

- Is there a clear, succinct mission statement that is not only current but also understood by all trustees?
- Is there a strategic plan and is there a process in place for periodic review of the plan?
- Have all facets of the school been considered when formulating the plan?
- Do "action items" include a funding mechanism? Is there a way to fund the vision?
- Does the board establish annual goals for itself?
- Do board members participate in professional development opportunities?

Selection and Composition

As discussed throughout this book, there is nothing more critical to the success of a school than the processes in place for the selection and composition of the board. In this category, the key questions include:

- What is the structure of the committee on trustees?
- Is the committee communicating with all board members?
- Does the committee have a matrix of prospective board members that identifies skills needed—both short-term and long-term?
- Is the size of the board a positive or a negative?
- Are all committees functioning and effective?
- Are the head of school and board chair included as ex-officio members of the committee?

Organization/Structure

How the board is organized reflects effectiveness in meeting the goals and objectives of the organization. The key questions include:

- Are the bylaws clear, concise, up-to-date, and followed?
- Is the committee structure of the board valuable in meeting the demands of the board and the needs of the school?
- Does the board seek ways to involve all constituencies of the school?
- Does the board recognize and act on the difference between their responsibilities and those of the school's administration?
- Overall, does the board understand its responsibilities?
- Are there individual trustees who are not effective in their role?
- Does the board review its work and is this process meaningful?

Orientation and Training

You hope that the committee on trustees has done an outstanding job in identifying and selecting trustees. Even so, there is more that must be done. Orientation as well as ongoing training and education will encourage trustees to focus on being the best they can be. The key questions in this category include:

- Is there a formal orientation session for all new trustees?
- Is there a board policy manual and does it include information useful to becoming familiar with the work of the board and the organization?
- Does the policy manual include a clear definition of conflict of interest and how the board addresses this issue?
- Is there a structured, formalized program for board education?
- Is funding available for board members to attend/ participate in professional development opportunities designed for the board?
- Does the board conduct an annual or periodic retreat as a way to explore a range of issues beneficial to both the board and the school?

Meetings

The issues surrounding meetings are more complex than perhaps initially believed. Meetings set the tone for a "board culture" that in many ways defines who board members are, what they believe is important, how they operate, and the impact they have. Questions regarding such issues as frequency and length, which should not be taken lightly, include:

- Is the current number of meetings per year about right? Are more needed and why? Are fewer needed and why?
- Do board meetings typically last longer than two hours?
- Is the agenda properly prepared and reviewed by the officers or executive committee prior to the meeting?
- Are the agenda and supporting documentation sent to board members prior to the board meeting?
- Do committees meet at intervals between board meetings?

- Is the staff liaison role understood and respected by board committees?
- Are committee reports effective and useful?
- Is financial information presented and conveyed in a manner that non-financial people can easily understand?

Individual Trustees

Each individual trustee plays a significant role as a part of the board of trustees. The board is no better than its worst trustee. Therefore, because each trustee is a key member of the board, the manner in which each trustee does his or her job is essential. The key questions for the specific trustee are:

- Is the board member prepared for both committee and board meetings?
- Does the member capably perform assigned as well as volunteered responsibilities?
- Does the board member recommend others to serve on the board?
- Does the board member give as generously as possible?
- Does the board member recommend donors and solicit support?
- Does the board member respect the work of the entire board?
- Does the board member fully embrace and defend issues such as confidentiality and conflict of interest?

Head of School

The relationship between the head of school, the board chair, and the entire governing board is critical to the health and sustainability of the school. The key questions that support this relationship include:

- Does the board support the head and view his or her role as one of partnership and collaboration?
- Does the head establish annual goals that reflect the mission and vision of the school?
- Does the board have in place a fair and helpful way to evaluate the work of the head?
- Is the evaluation presented in a way that demonstrates respect for the work performed by the head and the staff?
- Does the board provide in the budget continuing education and professional development opportunities for the head?

* * *

Boards that do the best job of evaluating their own work are boards that embrace this as a key to being the best board possible. In such cases the school thrives because the vision shared by the key constituencies will result in a dynamic, thriving, vigorous, *and* sustainable independent or faith-based school!

CASE STORY #16
The Challenge of Communication

The question was a good one—it was raised to get a sense of what worked best. There was no hidden agenda and no thought given to hijacking the issue. As the chair of the board, Steven was well within his authority to seek the opinion on the matter from his new but very experienced head of school. Was there a way to determine board value and success as that issue relates to the number of meetings held each year? What was the specific relevance about meeting bi-monthly, quarterly, or on some other schedule?

It was a question raised during the search process. At the time Sharon, then a candidate for the position, had responded by indicating what the practice was at her current school. She made two things very clear to Steven. First, she believed that quarterly meetings were the best practice because that schedule allowed the standing committees to function by holding meetings at least once between each of the quarterly board meetings. Second, quarterly board meetings meant that the school's staff had time to prepare for these meetings and the committee meetings but did not place an undue burden of always preparing for board and committee meetings. Third, this schedule provided the board with the best possible avenue to focus on strategic issues rather operational ones. Sharon felt very strongly that this model was efficient, meaningful, and fostered the best possible relationship between the board and staff.

Steven stated that the school, for the past several years, had been meeting bi-monthly. This every-other-month schedule seemed to be working, and most of the board members seemed to be content with it. He admitted that it did make scheduling committee meetings around board meetings a bit of a challenge.

Sharon replied that while she preferred the quarterly meeting schedule, she would be glad to adjust to bi-monthly meetings should she be the successful candidate.

A few weeks later Steven called to inform Sharon that she had been selected as the new head of school. She was thrilled, and they discussed various employment details. Over the next few weeks they talked several times over a variety of issues. Eventually the conversation came back around to the number of board meetings the school would have per year. Steven informed Sharon that the decision had been made to change to quarterly meetings. Naturally, she assumed that Steven had discussed this with the full board and that all trustees, either by vote or consensus, had agreed with Steven's recommendation to switch to quarterly board meetings.

After Sharon had moved to the community where the organization was located, she and Steven began to prepare for the first meeting. In preparation she initiated meetings with individual board members, typically over lunch or coffee. During some of these conversations, she began to sense that the issue of the number of board meetings was not universally embraced or understood. She also sensed some resentment toward Steven for the manner in which this decision had been made. Apparently at a board meeting prior to Sharon's arrival, Steven announced that beginning after her arrival the board would switch from bi-monthly to quarterly meetings. Further, his announcement strongly hinted that this change was highly recommended by Sharon—almost sounding as if it were a condition of employment. Sharon was stunned.

Soon after that, she scheduled a meeting with Steven to find out exactly what the story was. She made sure he understood that their earlier conversation was just a dialogue about possibilities. While she favored quarterly meetings, she would be fine with bi-monthly meetings until such a time when the issue could be properly reviewed. Steven dismissed her concerns and in effect said that as the chair of the board, it was his prerogative to make these types of decisions. She wanted to say something about consensus and team building but decided it would not be prudent to do so. Just as she was getting to know the trustees this issue had put something of a dark cloud over her; she wanted Steven to know that she was being partly blamed for the decision. Sharon was troubled that there was a very definite communication challenge that needed to be addressed.

Questions for Discussion

1. *What does this encounter tell you about Steven and Sharon's relationship?*
2. *What does this encounter reveal about Steven's relationship with the board?*
3. *What is your opinion of Sharon's case for quarterly board meetings?*
4. *What factors or circumstances should be considered when deciding the correct number of meetings to have?*
5. *What correlation is there between the number of board meetings and the board doing the best possible job of governing the school?*
6. *What does this situation say about Steven's leadership style?*
7. *How do you believe board members should have reacted to the way in which this was communicated?*
8. *How should this type of change result in a need to alter the bylaws?*
9. *What does this story say regarding collaboration and trust?*
10. *How should this matter have been resolved?*

Chapter Eighteen

◆

Surviving Versus Thriving: Why Some Boards Struggle Where Others Succeed

For independent and faith-based schools' boards, simply surviving is not a strategy but rather an excuse not to address the limitations and current inabilities keeping them from thriving. Loss of focus and direction does happen, but recognizing the board is in a downward spiral should not mean circumstances can't be improved. The board can become vibrant and thriving. Addressing these eight issues will return the board to what is most helpful and productive. Boards can evolve from struggling to thriving by positively reflecting on what has led to current circumstances and taking the steps that will make a difference.

1. **Ineffective or Poor Leadership**

   Struggling: As almost every independent and faith-based school knows, everything rises and falls on the effectiveness of the leadership. A weak and uninspiring board chair or board member will greatly diminish the board's ability to carry out its responsibilities. The board and school will suffer if recognizable and dynamic leadership is not present.

Thriving: Trustees and especially the committee on trustees must recognize that board leadership—the chair and other board officers—must be selected and encouraged to take on the responsibilities of leadership roles. As board members demonstrate through their skills and abilities, the committee will recognize these characteristics and thus encourages them to accept leadership roles on the board of trustees.

2. **Deficiency in the Selection Process**

Struggling: It is imperative that the board's committee on trustees performs its primary responsibilities of identifying, recruiting, securing, orienting, and educating the individuals most likely to make a positive difference on the board.

Thriving: The trustee selection process ranks near the very top of what will determine the effectiveness of the board and therefore the school. The committee on trustees, all trustees, and the head of school must be involved in the entire trustee selection process. Intentionality and a process intended to reveal best practices are what must be in place to ensure the best possible trustees are considered.

3. **Lack of Commitment and Understanding of Roles and Responsibilities**

Struggling: This issue, of course, is directly related to number two above. If the board members individually or collectively do not grasp and embrace their role, it is the responsibility of the committee on trustees as well as the board's leadership (officers) to turn the board in the direction of its proper role, identify the board's priorities, and lead a discussion of what commitment means.

Thriving: While commitment to serving on the board might have been a priority, individual circumstances change and allegiance to best practices diminishes. Trustees become ineffective or difficult. This may show up as a lack of attendance or disengagement when present. Thriving boards have a process they can turn to that allows them to alter the course and move forward. This can often be found in the effective utilization of educational opportunities for board members.

4. **Insufficient or the Absence of Ongoing Board Education**

   Struggling: Professional development opportunities must be not only available to trustees but considered a mandatory responsibility. Annual retreats as well as other opportunities to educate the board will lead to a more engaged and committed board and one that accepts its responsibilities.

   Thriving: With few exceptions, every independent and faith-based school board should engage in ongoing education. Board retreats, orientation sessions, webinars, books, blogs, etc. should all be considered as a part of what it means to be a trustee. The committee on trustees, board chair, and head of school should all play a part in making sure these opportunities are available to board members. All too often there is the assumption that every trustee knows everything there is to know about being a trustee at the school. Sometimes there is the belief that since board members are often men and women in powerful positions of responsibility, they already possess an innate knowledge of what it means to be a trustee of an independent school. Rarely is this actually the case.

5. **Failure to Utilize the Skills and Talents That Exist Within the Board**

   Struggling: It must be communicated to all board members not only how they can collectively support the school, but also how individuals' specific skills, experiences, and knowledge make them an asset to this board. If these things are not communicated to board members they may feel as if they are being underutilized and their contributions are not understood or appreciated. This will lead to lack of engagement and boredom.

   Thriving: Get to know trustees and make the most out of the relationship by being sure their areas of strength, skills, support, and interest are fully understood. Don't assume but rather specifically ask a board member to assist with a project or task that is suited to his or her interest or skill level. In almost every case, the board member will appreciate being called on to serve.

6. **Failure to Communicate with and within the Board**

   Struggling: Every leader understands the value and importance of communication. When it is lacking, there is a tendency to substitute what may or may not be accurate information. This type of environment allows for unwanted gossip and rumors to thrive. The ability to continually craft the message for the board to manage its work and provide the best possible governance is critical. Communication, or the absence thereof, has more to do with creating a struggling board environment than perhaps almost any other issue.

Thriving: Regular or periodic communication is a key factor for maintaining a level of engagement with the board. Not only board meetings and committee meetings, but other forms of engagement such as special events or dinner for board members and spouses reinforce the idea that the board is important and very worthy of the investment the school makes in the process of maintaining a healthy board and therefore a healthy school!

7. **Absence of a Strategic Vision for the School**

Struggling: Lack of vision is a killer for the school and signals to the constituencies that there is not much going on in terms of setting the school's future. Articulating a compelling vision is the joint responsibility of the board and the school's leadership. It is an important step to vitality and sustainability.

Thriving: The question the school's constituencies often ask is, "What is the vision of the school?" In other words, is there a strategic plan and, if so, how will the plan get us where we want to be in five years? The board and the head of school must be able to articulate a compelling response to ensure and reassure everyone connected with the school that there is a goal and plan, and that the board and leadership are in a strong position to move the process forward.

8. **Failure to Work in Support or Partnership with the Head of School**

Struggling: One of the most important components of a school is the relationship between the governing board and the head of school, including senior staff leadership. This partnership is without question the difference between excellence and success or mediocrity and failure.

Thriving: Supporting the head of school may be the single greatest responsibility of the board. Creating and sustaining a culture of support will do much to ensure the head has the confidence to carry out his or her responsibilities in that role. If supportive, inspiring, and encouraging leadership is the key factor in determining the viability of a school, then this factor is at the pinnacle of what it means to be the best board member possible.

* * *

To be certain, there are other factors that every independent school board must face when striving to create and maintain a best-practices board. However, these fundamental concepts cannot be overlooked by a board looking for ways and methods to improve and to serve the school as effectively as possible.

CASE STORY #17
Intentionally Choosing to Ignore Best Practices

Ben enjoyed conducting workshops for independent and faith-based schools in which both board members and heads of schools attended and participated in the discussions. Hearing the same information at the same time would lead to conversations regarding best practices, and that would result in stronger leadership and more meaningful experiences for the school's students. When the call came to lead a workshop for trustees and heads of schools, Ben was ready to go!

The workshop took place at a well-known and respected school, and the state independent school association was an active advocate for bringing together these groups. There were about sixty participants representing fifteen schools. Each school was represented by the head of school and two or more board members. It was an ideal opportunity to discuss a range of issues that would benefit the head and trustees as well as serve to strengthen their relationship while defining their different roles.

The workshop went well, and Ben was thrilled with the issues that were raised and the ensuing discussions that took place. It was exactly what you want in such a workshop. One school, Northwood Christian Academy, brought their head of school, the board chair, and two additional trustees. They were engaged and made every indication of understanding key issues. Brenda, the head of school, was in her second year. She shared that there had been some issues in the past with an inability to separate what the board's role is and how it differs from that of the head. She saw it as a very positive sign to have the chair and two trustees attend the workshop.

About a year later Ben received a call from Brenda. She related that although the trustees who attended the workshop had been receptive and understood the issues, once they returned to the school, they began to regress and slip back into old habits. Ben asked her to describe an issue that would serve as an example of the board's actions. Brenda then shared the story of hiring the head, or principal, of the upper school. This individual had been on the job for a few months when something happened to upset a trustee. The issue involved the trustee's child and rose to the level that this trustee was convinced the upper school principal should be fired. Unfortunately, the trustee happened to be the chair of the board at Northwood. Brenda was at the point of resigning as head.

On a positive note, Brenda was able to convince the chair to allow Ben to conduct a retreat on the general topic of trustee responsibilities. Brenda asked Ben to focus on the fundamental concept that an independent or faith-based school has one employee—the head of school. All other employees report directly or indirectly to the head of school. Ben agreed that he would be direct but encouraging as he made this point clear during the retreat.

When Ben arrived at the retreat, he certainly remembered the chair from the workshop he had conducted a year earlier. They had a good reunion, and Ben was convinced that the chair was a reasonable person who understood that this issue with the upper school principal should not, in fact, be taken up by the board of trustees.

Ben wrapped up the retreat and talked with Brenda on the way to the airport. She felt good about the discussion and hopeful that the board had recognized that this was a management and operational concern and not an issue for the board. They promised to stay in touch. Their initial communications were mostly affirmative indicating the board seemed to be "getting it."

About six months later, Brenda sent an e-mail to Ben stating that the board had done a reversal and again demanded that she terminate the upper school principal. Brenda even went so far as to say that the board was aware that this was not best practice and that Ben would be distraught at the board's action, but in the end they didn't care. The board was convinced that they were different and had to intervene to save the school.

In the end, Brenda resigned, and the board fired the upper school principal. A few months later, Brenda contacted Ben indicating she had been appointed head of school at a wonderful school in another state. And she further confirmed that she was confident and encouraged by what looked like a board who genuinely understood their role. Time would tell, but Ben wanted to be optimistic and congratulated Brenda on her appointment.

Questions for Discussion

1. *Why is this a recurring issue for trustees?*
2. *Should the head allow the board to have input into hiring faculty and staff?*
3. *Why is comingling of responsibilities such a dangerous approach to the operation of an independent or faith-based school?*
4. *What kind of head should Northwood expect to hire?*
5. *Will this be a revolving door—a new head every two to three years?*
6. *If board professional development does not seem to work, what can the administration do?*
7. *Is there a role for accrediting organizations? What about intervention from the state independent school organizations?*

Chapter Nineteen

◆

Addressing the Issue of Ineffective or Difficult Board Members

Serving on the board of trustees is an honor that comes with certain responsibilities as well expectations for the work that should be done. Each trustee must accept that premise to be effective and committed to that role. Then why is it that far too many independent schools, faith-based schools, or any nonprofit organizations for that matter have a few board members who make the work of the board extremely difficult? The board's job and the head's job come with enough challenges and issues not to have the additional burden of a few board members who refuse to work for the greater good. These board members have little regard for teamwork and best practices and view the word through lenses that view only their interests.

There are at least eight characteristics, or traits, that can be identified that constitute characteristics of ineffective board members. Identifying these traits is the first step towards a healthier board and a healthier school. It will fall to the committee on trustees, the board chair and ultimately the entire board to address the problems presented by difficult board members.

Eight Traits of Ineffective or Difficult Board Members

1. **They rarely attend board and committee meetings.**

   At first glance, this may not be considered a difficult trait, but upon reflection, a lack of respect for the work of the board and a lack of engagement in the process suggests that these board members believe other priorities are more important than attendance at board and committee meetings.

   Certainly there are circumstances or schedule conflicts that cause board members to occasionally miss a meeting. However, when missing meetings becomes the norm, then the board has a problem that will have to addressed. Depending on how often the board meets, it may be up to six months before a board member is present again. Chronic absence is a problem. Written into the bylaws of many schools are statements regarding what to do when board members miss a certain number of meetings. While this language is good, it is also almost universally ignored. The key is always in the trustee recruitment phase and setting this as an expectation for every new board member.

2. **When attending meetings they are not engaged or do not actively participate in the discussions.**

   There is a big difference between attentive listening and a lack of participation. These are the folks who whisper to other board members or who stare at their phones and clearly ignore what is going in the meeting. One might argue that this is better than other much worse traits, but this trait is another type of distraction that creates unnecessary anxiety (primarily to the chair) and, if allowed to continue, begins to set up a culture that tolerates such behavior. Eventually, this will poison the board in such a way that good board prospects will say no to the opportunity to join the board. While seemingly a benign trait on the surface, it has the potential to set the tone for an unhealthy board environment.

3. **They micromanage school operations even though this completely contradicts best practices.**

This trait is a complex and extremely troubling characteristic that reveals itself in all manner of settings that have nothing to do with governance issues. In many cases the board members understand their role until something comes up that they believe personally affects them or their child attending the school. Parental involvement is welcomed, but parental interference is not. And board members too often side with their parent friend as opposed to doing the right but difficult thing. It is here that an important reminder is appropriate: board members have no power and no authority as trustees when acting individually and not as part of an official board or committee meeting.

4. **They have an agenda that moves the board away from its mission and strategy.**

There is recognition that almost all board members join the board with particular interests and aspects of the school that they wish to champion. That is certainly acceptable. The line is crossed, though when trustees take their interests and move them in such a direction that it pushes other needs and priorities to the side. In other words, their needs are more important and they know what is in the best interest of the school. There are numerous examples of this but consider this one, which reveals why it can be such a problem:

A board member is the mother of a daughter in the school, and that student is artistic and participates in all school plays. Unfortunately, the school does not have an adequate theatre, but it is something that will be considered as the school looks strategically at what facility and space needs to consider. This is not good enough for this board member parent. After being told by both the head of school and board chair that a theatre is not a short-term goal, she begins to lobby other theatre parents in an attempt to force her will and get her way. Both the head and chair are forced to step in and say enough is enough. Micromanaging, lobbying parents, criticizing the head and the board for their lack of vision is inappropriate behavior and has no place on the board. Strategic thinking and planning for what is in the best long-term interest of the school should always be the priority.

5. **They have no problem with hijacking meetings to promote their issue.**

There is a reason that an agenda is prepared and approved for each board meeting. Agendas are designed to keep the board focused on the task at hand as opposed to being sidetracked and taken away from defined priorities to whatever is on the mind of individual trustees. The simple, direct solution is that the chair of the board should in no way allow or tolerate such actions that represent one or two trustees. But when you are trying to work with peers who believe the world revolves around their next statement, it makes for a challenging and disruptive environment. It's not all about you. It's about how I can lead by serving, how I can set aside what I want for what is best for the school, and how I can be a part of team that wants to enhance the school. Culture encourages behavior and behavior leads to actions.

6. **They seek to intimidate (bully) the school's staff and even other board members.**

While this is somewhat rare, it does happen. And when it does the consequences are severe. This trait comes primarily from trustees who view the world as being all about them, who have no wish to serve as a team player, who talk but rarely listen, and who have no regard for strategic direction. Ironically, these individuals will deny all of the above, claiming that they are acting in what they believe is in the best of the school. Of course, such behavior is in complete defiance of what is acceptable and what is considered best practice.

Such board members seem to have little concern about directly approaching a staff member with whatever their issues might be. They have no regard for protocol or organizational hierarchy. One of the fundamental truths for board members is that they have only one employee—the head of school. Trustees have no authority over members of the school's faculty or staff. However, there are trustees who refuse to accept this. Perhaps it is because a board culture has allowed this attitude to take root. And then there are those board members who have no problem alarming other trustees by their behavior, demeanor, and attitude. All, of course, under the guise of what is best for the school.

7. **They ignore fundamental board precepts such as maintaining confidentiality and avoiding conflicts of interest.**

   Board leadership should take the steps necessary to communicate the importance of confidentiality and explain the dangers of conflicts of interest. Concern seeps in when the school encounters trustees who believes that these rules do not apply to them. Confidentiality is critical because the board may be discussing sensitive issues that are intended only for the board to hear. Society seems to no longer believe in the importance of confidentiality. Perhaps the pendulum has swung more in the direction of transparency without realizing that transparency has it limits. There are appropriate places where it should be acceptable not to reveal things in order to protect the integrity of board discussions.

   Conflict of interest becomes an issue when a trustee's motives come into question. There are certain circumstances when there is a conflict of interest and the board is aware of the nature of that conflict. Again, what are the motivations of board members, and do their actions reflect a spirit of character and integrity? Or are board members attempting to hide something that the board would not wish to be a part of? Every list of expectations and every board orientation discussion should include a thorough review of these types of issues to ensure complete clarity as well as an understanding of the consequences that come from a lack of confidentiality or conflicts of interest.

8. **They work in secret, attempting to manipulate people and circumstances.**

   Board members, while often meaning well, do not grasp the concept that they have no authority as trustees unless they are participating in an official board or committee meeting. Unfortunately, too often board members are not aware of this concept and have no problem believing that it is acceptable to discuss board business with a few other trustees, or perhaps with no other trustees at all. Of course, there are those trustees who are not concerned about this and believe such conversations are in the best interest of the school.

There are numerous examples of this happening when board members have an agenda that is in opposition to the identified strategic direction of the school. Invariably this behavior is about mobilizing support for whatever their particular issues are. Should the board chair become aware of this activity, he or she must step in and remind all trustees what constitutes acceptable behavior and best practices. This becomes especially toxic when one or two board members come to believe that the head is no longer effective so these members push their personal agenda for a change by wrongfully and inappropriately discussing board business.

The idea of attempting to manipulate others in a one-on-one exchange is unethical and lethal to the idea of the board partnering with the head of school. If such a change must be made, there are appropriate ways to accomplish this. Board members may get together as friends, as parents, as fellow alumni, etc., but when conversations turn to governance or issues related to the work of the board, that is when a problem surfaces. What may appear to be innocent can sometimes turn into something destructive. What board members are truly seeking what is best for the school and who have a personal agenda with little regard for what the school needs?

Strategies for Dealing with Ineffective or Problem Board members

Fortunately, there are strategies and tactics for addressing ineffective and problem board members. Of course, the most effective strategy can be found in the selection process when the head of school and the committee on trustees can work together to ensure that prospective trustees are vetted in such a way that the best candidates can emerge and lead the way to a brighter future for the school. Yet, in almost every independent and faith-based school, there are board members who are ineffective, difficult, and not concerned with best practices. What can be done?

Provided here are five strategies that the board chair and board can adopt to help to reorient board members to doing the work they were called to do.

Strategy One

The board chair must accept responsibility for managing ineffective or difficult board members. When identifying board chair responsibilities, this is often overlooked because it is considered negative. The practical matter is that the board chair does not want to take on any responsibility for disciplining or correcting the actions or behavior of other board members. This is true for several reasons. They are peers, volunteering their time to the school. They may be personal friends or professional colleagues who work in the same or similar businesses. Therefore, it becomes a challenge for the chair and a potential threat to the board member.

Strategy Two

In many cases, the problem can be resolved with a one-on-one conversation between the chair and the trustee. The matter is addressed and resolved without anyone else knowing about this private conversation. Keep in mind, often the action or behavior is not intentional but rather simply not knowing or understanding what best practices looks like. This conversation, while potentially difficult, will greatly reduce or eliminate further such actions by trustees. Face-to-face discussions are always preferred in circumstances like these. For more minor transgressions, a phone call or e-mail might be all that is needed.

Strategy Three

Utilize the opportunities that ongoing board education or board retreats provide. Continuous review of best practices is never a bad investment in this key constituency; it is time well spent. Board education programs as well as board retreats allow the school to focus on a few specific issues that may be of concern, or they may focus on more broad areas of responsibilities. Workshops, seminars, conferences, and other methods of delivery are examples of professional development that allow the board to become more familiar with best practices and gain a better understanding of what is and is not a proper role for the board.

There are numerous professional development organizations at the local, state, regional, and national level that provide these types of educational opportunities. Board retreats are excellent venues to have an outside, independent facilitator meet with the board to discuss of a range of issues. This is beneficial to the board as well as for the relationship between the board and head. A common reason for a retreat is some disagreement that has emerged between the head and the board over one or more issues usually having to do with areas of responsibility.

Strategy Four

The school should include in its bylaws both term limits and finite tenure a trustee may serve on the board before rolling off. Schools that have neither and an inability to incorporate other strategies may find themselves with a long-term problem board member. Term limits and tenure are not the ideal solution to this problem. They are, however, effective in eventually removing a problem board member. Many independent and faith-based schools have term limits—typically a three-year term with one additional three-year term. In most schools, the second term has become automatic without any discussion about whether or not the board member has been an effective, engaged, and contributing member or not.

Again, the fear of offending someone is more powerful than the concern for what is in the best interest of the school. And who decides what criteria should be used to determine this? This is why documents like a covenant agreement can be a method to help make this determination. Term limits without finite tenure are useless. Ongoing three-year terms with no end in sight mean that board service has the potential to be a life sentence for both the board and the board member. The bylaws should be clear in stating the number of terms that can potentially be served before rolling off. Board members should roll off for at least one year, if not longer.

Strategy Five

Have the most effective onboarding, or orientation process possible. An undeniable responsibility for both the head of school and the committee on trustees is to put together a board orientation program that is practical and meaningful. This orientation should set the tone for future board actions and behavior, and it should put every new trustee on notice as to what constitutes best practice. Setting boundaries as it relates to "do's and don'ts" is critical to having a genuinely healthy board—and a board with fewer ineffective or difficult board members. From a practical standpoint, new trustees should set aside half a day for the orientation. The session should include remarks from the chair, head, and trustee committee chairs. More on orientation may be found in Appendix E.

* * *

It is a given at some point that every independent and faith-based school board is going to have to acknowledge and address ineffective and difficult board members. Even healthy boards must face this reality. Develop the best possible strategy, do what needs to be done, and learn and grow from the experience.

CASE STORY #18
Where Do Your Trustees' Children Attend School?

Joan and her husband Tom shook hands with the head of school and exchanged several minutes of pleasantries. Elliott, the head, knew Joan because she was a trustee, but he had never met Tom. Elliott, although anxious to get to the point of the meeting, wanted to break the ice with Tom and spend some time exploring his experiences, background, etc. Of course, Elliott was well aware of why the meeting was taking place and eager to put his powers of persuasion to the test.

A few days earlier Joan had sent Elliott a detailed e-mail outlining the reason why they were seriously considering taking their children out of Westview Academy. They had two children who attended the school—a fifth grader and an eighth grader. Elliott knew from experience that these were the two grade levels when families who considered opting out of a K–12 school were more likely to do so.

Joan's e-mail described bullying issues upsetting their fifth grader and academic issues with their older child. As they sat down to discuss the matter, Elliott carefully listened to the two parents describe their concerns calmly but with purpose. While Joan and Tom seemed to be genuinely wrestling with their decision, it was increasingly clear to Elliott that they would likely be leaving the school. Elliott expressed concern with the issues they raised and promised he would meet with the head of the lower school to seek a resolution. Neither Joan nor Tom had met with anyone (teachers or administrators) to communicate problems regarding their children. When Elliott later went to the head of the middle school, he seemed very surprised, confessing he was unaware of any problems their students were having.

Following the meeting Elliott wrote the couple a note indicating his appreciation for their willingness to articulate concerns and consider staying at Westview. But one thought he kept coming back to was this: Since Joan was a board member, shouldn't she be inclined to seek a way to work through the issues that she had described? After all, don't trustees have a unique relationship with the school that suggests that there should be a pathway to work through such issues? Perhaps they would make the decision to stay and discover ways to resolve the issues with their children. Little did Elliott realize that there was a much larger issue just waiting to blow up.

About a week later Joan and Tom sent Elliott an e-mail stating that after thoughtful and prayerful consideration they had decided that their children would not be returning to Westview. Joan apologized for being late in notifying him of their decision. They admitted to being torn but felt the decision was in everyone's best interest. Elliott reflected, "not everyone's—certainly not the school's!" And then as he read on, there it was. Joan indicated that her decision to withdraw her two children in no way would impact her continuing to serve on the board. To say that he was astounded by this statement was a profound understatement.

Over the course of his career Elliott had engaged in numerous professional conversations with colleagues about the issue of whether or not parents should continue to serve on the board when they have made a conscious decision to withdraw their children from the school. He clearly understood there were exceptions including certain learning differences or when the children were not a good fit with the school. However, best practices were widely interpreted to assume that any parent/trustee making such a decision would immediately resign as a trustee. The symbolism of serving as a board member at one school while your children attend another school was widely viewed as unacceptable.

Elliott pondered how he should respond to her extraordinary communication. What would be his strategy to address the matter? There was no way he was going to allow the status quo to be acceptable. He quickly decided that his next step would be a conversation with Karen, the chair of the board. His relationship with her was strong and one built on trust, respect, and open lines of communication. He was confident that she would be very surprised and concerned by this turn of events.

A few days later Karen and Elliott sat down to discuss the situation. Elliott had done some research and was prepared for the conversation that was about to take place. Basically, he had learned pretty much what he already knew. Best practices strongly suggested that any board member who withdrew their children from an independent school should voluntarily step down from serving on the board. It was an understood rule of thumb, but was it more than that? However, he was confident that Karen would agree and that she would be willing to discuss the matter with Joan.

Questions for Discussion

1. *Why do independent schools take this issue so seriously?*
2. *Should the head of school be more aware of the issues/ concerns described by the parents?*
3. *Was the head right or wrong to research the issue?*
4. *Why would the head approach the board chair on this matter?*
5. *When, if ever, is it appropriate for the board chair to intervene?*
6. *What would be the right outcome to this story?*
7. *How will this actually play out?*

Chapter Twenty

◆

Board Values That Matter Most

Whathat are the guiding principles that direct the board to act and behave in a certain way? How are these principles of independent and faith-based school governance articulated in a manner that brings clarity to the true purpose of their work? As a board, and as individuals on a board, what is my role for advancing the school and enhancing the board's culture to achieve something truly special?

The Governance Promise is comprised of six statements that speak directly to culture, values, attitude, behavior, and to reflection of the board's work. The ideas are not revolutionary but articulating them in this way reflects a recognition and understanding that addresses the fundamental work of the board of trustees as well as the most meaningful way to carry out its responsibilities. It is the capstone covenant that defines the board of trustees.

Promise One

As a trustee, I promise to uphold an environment where support, trust, and respect are exhibited and adopted as the only way in which all business between the head of the school and the governing board is carried out.

Promise Two

As a trustee, I promise to maintain a distinctive, positive attitude in which the school thrives because of the partnership established between the leadership of the organization and the governing board. I am optimistic even though the school may be faced with adverse circumstances.

Promise Three

As a trustee, I promise to foster a welcoming spirit of cooperation in which the needs and priorities of the school will always prevail over my agenda or self-interest. I recognize that my voice should be tempered by the greater need of how can I best serve the school.

Promise Four

As a trustee, I promise that even under circumstances in which the school is under pressure to depart from its mission and goals, the relationship I have with the school's staff and other members of the governing board will remain steadfast, and I will work through whatever conflict or crisis exists.

Promise Five

As a trustee, I promise to support a culture in which transitions, such as those created when a new board chair is appointed, are seamless and come with little interruption to the head or the trustees.

Promise Six

As a trustee, I promise to make a commitment to being a best-practices board, reaching for the highest standards of innovation, professionalism, and excellence.

**

This is what being a trustee of an independent or faith-based school should be about. Having these statements as the standard on which the work of a trustee is based has the potential to impact the school in significant ways and create healthy governing boards.

CASE STORY #19
A Meaningful Evaluation of the Head

Greg was well into his third year as the head of a well-known and well-established independent school. His evaluation the first two years had been overwhelmingly positive. As a result, he received the maximum bonus provided for in his contract. He had been evaluated on agreed upon criteria established by the committee on the head that included the current board chair, the immediate past board chair, and the vice chair of the board. Most of the criteria centered on meeting budgetary numbers in terms of overall revenue, fundraising, and expense control. There were other factors, but the biggest concern was meeting the budget as the budget included programs and services the school provided.

The third year was different. Paul had risen through the ranks on the board and was now both vice chair and treasurer—an anomaly in the bylaws that Greg viewed with suspicion. In the spring of Greg's third year Paul scheduled a lunch meeting with him and Brenda, the board chair. The three discussed a variety of issues before Paul finally launched into his real agenda. He began by saying he did not like the way the last two evaluations had been conducted, and he was determined to do things differently this time. He shared with Greg an evaluation survey he was planning to provide all trustees. Greg was a little surprised because no survey had been used before. However, he indicated he had no problem with the trustees completing the survey. Greg was confident that the results would be favorable.

In Paul's next breath he stated that he was going to have Greg's leadership team also complete the survey. Greg looked at both Paul and Brenda, stunned by what he had just heard. He made it immediately clear he had concerns about this. He was a leader with high expectations that sometimes led to disagreements with some of the decisions that were made. He also knew his number one priority was to do what was best for the school, not to try to prevail in a popularity contest. Furthermore, these staff members reported to and worked with Greg—not with Paul and Brenda.

Greg made it clear he was concerned about having these senior administrators take the survey. Paul was direct in saying he was unconcerned with what Greg thought and was planning to meet with these staff members and provide them with the survey.

Three weeks later, Paul and Brenda asked Greg to resign. The decision was based in large part by what the staff had said. Greg was speechless. In less than a year he had gone from an evaluation in which he was praised for his vision, numerous accomplishments, and a genuine sense that the school was making huge strides . . . to a shameful and despicable ending to his tenure. Yes, Greg realized that some decisions were not popular and knew that the senior staff was not always in agreement. However, Greg always asked for and received their input, always listened to their perspective, and always respected their recommendations. In the end Paul had found a way to bring down Greg and get someone into the position that would do his bidding and reflect his priorities.

Questions for Discussion

1. *What is your opinion of Paul's methods?*
2. *Do you believe it is a best practice for an officer on a board of trustees to hold more than one office at a time?*
3. *Should the staff have been surveyed?*
4. *Why do you believe Brenda (the board chair) was not more vocal?*
5. *What do you believe motivated Paul?*

6. *What criteria do you believe should be measured as a part of Greg's evaluation?*

7. *What lessons would be most beneficial for Greg to learn?*

Chapter Twenty-One

◆

The Covenant Agreement: Signing Off on Fundamental Principles

The boards of nonprofit 501(c)(3) independent and faith-based schools have a legal as well as fiduciary responsibility to ensure that the schools thrive by living out their mission and vision. These boards take their role seriously and are capable of providing a great service to the schools they lead. While we all strive for the ideal, to have the possibility of working alongside individuals who want to lead by serving, who possess great attitude and skills, and who want to work in partnership with the school's leadership creates a very special environment.

How can you ensure that the board will embrace these issues and accept them as the way in which best practices become a part of the board's culture? Do you rely on a verbal understanding? Are the bylaws crafted in such a way as to speak to issues such as these? What document, if any, does the board sign signaling their belief, understanding, and support? The vast majority of independent and faith-based schools do not have a formal, documented understanding that articulates the focus of board responsibilities. Why is this the case? Many schools have the impression that expressing these responsibilities by having the board sign something is either insulting or unnecessary.

There is something genuine and fundamental that brings an element of authenticity when you are asked to sign a document signifying and establishing an agreement or covenant between and among the board and the school. Boards that insist on having a Covenant Agreement stipulating responsibilities are more likely to have supportive, engaged, and vibrant boards focusing on their work as opposed to boards that are being distracted by issues unrelated to their core responsibilities. What is included in the Covenant Agreement document?

This document addresses a range of issues that each and every trustee must agree to. Topics include:

- Understanding the school
- Financial support and philanthropic priority
- Involvement and support for fundraising activities
- Commitment to staying engaged
- Respect for the work and authority of the board
- Personal agendas
- Conflict of interest
- Confidentiality
- Adherence to the Governance Promise

For a sample of a Covenant Agreement, see Appendix G.

CASE STORY #20

Being on the Same Page During the Board Chair Transition

The week had been a good one—productive, informative, encouraging, and affirming. All of the hard work covering the last few weeks and months had been rewarded by a fantastic visit from the accrediting team. The strategic plan, which had been the basis on which the accrediting team made its recommendations, was a carefully thought out document that articulated a compelling vision for the next five years with a nod to even longer-term goals. This was noted in their report in which a verbal summary was given on their last day on site at the school.

Scott Sullivan was completing his third year as head of school. The school, a K–8 institution, was connected to a large church in the community. Both the school and church were well established and highly regarded. While the relationship between the two was not perfect, the overall communication was adequate and the relationship stable.

Scott's first two years had been incredibly happy and productive. The relationship he had with his board, and particularly the board chair, Brian Gregory, had been exceptional. It was this board chair that was primarily responsible for Scott's selection and election by the full board. But after two years as chair, it was time for Brian to step down. In his place, Terry Matthews was appointed. The third year was filled with challenges in that relationship. They simply did not see eye to eye. Nothing Scott could do seemed to be good enough.

This transition, from Brian to Terry, had not been a smooth one. Unfortunately the school's bylaws did not describe the process by which the successor would be chosen or elected. Sometimes it was the vice chair and other times not. Of course, Scott had been caught in the middle of this and did not want to appear to be in a position of taking sides.

Following the departure of the accrediting team, Terry asked to meet with Scott and informed him that they would be joined by the executive committee. Scott assumed that the topic would a "post-mortem" on how the accreditation visit had gone and what the next steps would be. Scott hoped the meeting would be short as the next morning would be eighth-grade graduation. When he arrived he immediately noticed six serious-looking faces staring back at him.

Terry got right to the point and informed Scott that she and the executive committee were not pleased with Scott's work and were asking for his resignation! Scott was shocked. He could not believe what he had just heard. In the jumble of emotions he thought about his family who had moved halfway across the country for him to take what appeared to be a very attractive position. After he partially collected himself he asked, why? Very little explanation was given other than he and the board were not on the same page and that some of the staff thought him to be too demanding. There was no documentation, no warning, and no effort to try and resolve differences.

Scott thought, *Couldn't you have waited until after graduation?* He then asked what was to happen regarding the next day's commencement. He assumed they would not want him to participate. Then came the next shock—yes, they did want him to preside at graduation but that would be his last day! Scott started to refuse, thinking this to be outrageous, but instead he indicated that he would participate because he did not want the special occasion to be tainted by his resignation.

This story has a happy ending. A few weeks after this debacle another head at a K–12 school found out how poorly Scott had been treated and had an opening as the head of the lower school. Scott very gratefully accepted this position, allowing him and his family to remain in the community.

The underlying cause of this nightmare was a chair who was unwilling to set aside a personal agenda and look carefully at what was best for the school. Schools undergoing the transition from one chair to the next sometimes have the unfortunate experience of going from one head to the next. Terry thought she could find someone better. She suffered from the "grass is always greener" philosophy and believed that the school could always find someone capable to serve as head. What she was probably seeking was someone who would agree with her agenda.

Questions for Discussion

1. *What is your greatest concern with this story?*
2. *What does this say about the stability of the board?*
3. *What can organizations do to better prepare for the transition from one chair to the next?*
4. *Why do some boards believe that they can take this type of drastic action with no documentation, no warning, and no recourse?*
5. *Had you been in Scott's situation, what would you have done to build a relationship with Terry?*
6. *What could Brian and Terry have done differently?*
7. *Why can't we put aside personal differences and focus on what is best for the organization?*
8. *Could different language in the bylaws have been helpful?*

Chapter Twenty-Two

◆

The Role of the Head
of School

The head of school has a complex job with many moving parts. It is a position of enormous responsibility and filled with challenges, opportunities, great joy, and occasional frustration. Being the head means that "the buck stops here" and that the burdens and joys of leadership fall on this person.

Among the many character traits that best serve people in this role is a level of self-awareness that sustains them in the midst of many situations and difficult circumstances. Do you understand your strengths and weaknesses? Have you participated in the various psychological inventories that determine the kind of leader you are or are likely to be? Are these characteristics ones that will serve you well as a head of school? Are there aspects of your behavior that may benefit from professional development opportunities or coaching? Do you know the type of leader you are and want to become? These factors, and many others, are part of your self-awareness inventory that will prepare you for the challenges of leadership, management, and administrative work you face as a head of school.

One of the most challenging responsibilities of the head is working directly with the governing board and board chair. For the new or first-time head it may well mean working with an unfamiliar but vital constituency. This is unchartered waters for most everyone who becomes a head. It is unlikely most first-time heads have participated in professional development opportunities that have focused on working with governing boards. In these settings, many questions arise, including:

- Do you understand the dynamics of this relationship?
- Are you prepared to now report to a group of volunteers?
- Are you prepared to be evaluated by the board?
- Do you have any experience in working with/reporting to a volunteer board?
- Who can advise you about this relationship?
- Do your professional associations and organizations provide professional development opportunities?
- How well do you know the board chair and do you realize the importance of your professional relationship with this person?

These and other questions are just the beginning of what it is like to be a head at an independent or faith-based school. Where do you begin and what are your priorities when it comes to this relationship? In your first ninety days the following should be your priority as you begin to build a relationship with the board of trustees:

1. Establish a Relationship the Board Chair

This relationship should be built on the seven most needed important characteristics:

- Collaboration and communication
- Respect
- Trust
- Support
- Attitude
- Shared vision
- Leadership
- Self-awareness

Establish a specific time to meet one-on-one. You should consider meeting once a week or every two weeks to sit down and discuss important issues impacting the school. A breakfast or lunch may be just the right setting to establish this relationship. Consider somewhere away from the campus or a location other than the school as this will allow for fewer interruptions and more candid dialogue. This ongoing dialogue may include big ideas and small ones. It should include strategy and tactics as well as any issue that the chair may need a "heads up" about. While day-to-day issues are not a priority, trustees and board chairs do not look too kindly on big surprises. Keep the chair informed about your activities, priorities, and what you see ahead as opportunities and challenges.

2. Build a Relationship with Each Trustee

Seeing and even working with board members at board and committee meetings is only a part of getting to know the individuals on your board. These are effective tactics you can employ to develop relationships with trustees:

- As you begin your role as head of school and as your time as the head continues, establishing and building on relationships with the school's trustees is critical. Over time, trustees come and go so building relationships with every board member is a continuous process.

- Meet with each individual trustee. Make an appointment at a location most convenient with the trustee and spend one-on-one time. Discover their interests—vocation, family, likes and dislikes, leisure activities, and anything that demonstrates your genuine interest in who they are. While this may be an opportunity for them to get to know you, the real matter at hand is making sure they know that you are interested in getting to know them.

- Seek out board members at events. Every school has events throughout the year. This is an ideal opportunity to look for trustees and engage them in a brief conversation—including the opportunity to thank them for attending the event. Of course, trustees are likely attending a school event because of their child's involvement.

3. Develop Networking Opportunities

Look for ways to build relationships with other heads. Conferences, workshops, and meetings at the local, regional, and national level are all excellent ways to foster these connections. The ability to communicate with someone you have gotten to know regarding a particular issue is an enormously important way to expand your knowledge of that issue.

4. Participate in Professional Development

Seek learning opportunities that are directed toward both the head and board chair. Being with other head/board chair teams is a unique way to share ideas and discuss challenges and ways to enhance and deepen this relationship. Participating in such opportunities together, the head will better understand the board chair's role, and it will certainly enlighten the board chair as to the head's responsibilities.

5. Have a "Trustee Recognition Day" at your School

This can take a variety of forms, but setting aside one day a year to encourage staff, volunteers, and other constituencies to express appreciation to the board members for their volunteer service and leadership is a reminder as to why they are on the board and will perhaps inspire them to stay focused and engaged in their roles and responsibilities as trustees. It is also important for trustees to find occasions to thank the staff and volunteers.

* * *

Jim Rohn's well-known quote concerning leadership is a reminder that the head of school has a unique role and responsibility within the structure of the school:

> *The challenge of leadership is to be strong, but not rude; be kind, but not weak; be bold, but not bully; be thoughtful, but not lazy; be humble, but not timid; be proud, but not arrogant; have humor, but without folly.*

Schools require great leaders and inspired boards! The impact that these schools have on society and culture necessitates nothing less than our very best. The days ahead must be even better than the days behind!

CASE STORY #21
Being Derailed by One Issue

The retreat had gone well—which was somewhat of a surprise. The school's board of trustees could be difficult to work with and even more difficult to understand. So much was going well and the strategic direction had resulted in some amazing gains—enrollment, fundraising, student profile, faculty morale, and more. While everyone connected with the school should have been feeling very good, there were a handful of trustees whose agenda did not recognize that the head's leadership and performance was not only satisfactory, but also outstanding.

Toward the end of the retreat the discussion turned to an issue with the accounts receivable. Accounts receivable is a challenge at many schools for a variety of reasons. However, every school recognizes the importance of having as minimal a balance of accounts receivable as possible. Barton Academy was no different. The school was well respected with a student population of approximately eight hundred. Enrollment was stable but growing, and this had not always been the case. The new head and his team had done much to re-energize the school, and morale was very high among certain members of the board.

The question at the retreat then came; "What is our current balance in accounts receivable?" The vice president for business cleared her throat and proclaimed, "We recognize this has been something of a troubling issue, but we are addressing it, and we have seen some very positive gains in the last few months." As these words were coming out of her mouth, a hand shot up and a new trustee, who was a former head of school, stated, "I think anything that is not very close to a zero balance is unacceptable.

During my time as a head of school, we rarely had this as an issue. What I am hearing about Barton is a huge concern." And there it was—his comments were momentarily met with bewildered silence. But within a few seconds the other trustees erupted at the vice president for business insisting that more should be done—and done immediately. The mood changed completely and quickly; the board became hostile, combative, and frustrated by what they were hearing. The former head had altered the atmosphere in the room without understanding the backstory of why the school had adopted the earlier strategy.

What neither the current board of trustees nor the former head of school knew was that years earlier the board had used receivables as an enrollment management strategy—a way to provide certain families with the ability to fund their children's education. In a sense, Barton Academy was serving as a benevolent creditor. At the time, everyone in the school's leadership accepted this strategy as policy and knew the result would be a higher than normal accounts receivable balance. Although there were a few remaining trustees from that time still on the board, they said nothing to support the vice president for business—knowing full well they were "throwing her under the bus."

The new treasurer and chair of the finance committee expressed shock that the school was in this situation. He demanded a complete review and a plan to eliminate as quickly as possible the accounts receivable issue. One of his first acts, without the knowledge of Barton's head or vice president for business, was to contact the auditor to gain additional insight into the matter. Unfortunately, because this auditor had little knowledge of the strategic use of need-based tuition assistance as an enrollment management issue, he proclaimed the school was out of control, and the vice president for business and head should be held accountable for resolving this matter.

The next several months included many difficult meetings in which there was a lot of talking and very little listening. This resulted in significant micromanaging and unethical behavior on the part of the board—including demanding to know who was receiving tuition assistance and making certain they were expelled for any lack of adherence to the policy regardless of circumstances.

Questions for Discussion

1. *Why had the former head of school made his statement without an understanding of the unique circumstances that led to the higher than normal accounts receivable balance?*
2. *Why did the board react in such a hostile manner?*
3. *What are some of the reasons that the few trustees who knew about and had voted for the enrollment management strategy said nothing when the issue surfaced?*
4. *Why did the treasurer not inform the head or vice president for business about the conversation with the auditor?*
5. *Should the head and/or vice president for business have spoken up at the retreat to explain the earlier strategy?*
6. *What does this story say about the relationship between the board, the head, and the vice president for business?*
7. *How should this story play out?*
8. *What relationship issues need to be addressed for the outcome to be positive?*

Chapter Twenty-Three

◆

Evaluating the Head:
Developing a Supportive
and Encouraging Process

It comes with a mixture of dread and anticipation, but less often does it come with support, encouragement, and recognition for a job well done. The process by which the head of school is evaluated by the board of trustees is one in which there is little continuity, consistency, or a sense of fairness. It is more a process of what the head has *not* achieved as opposed to celebrating what has been accomplished often in challenging circumstances. The reasons for this unfortunate phenomenon are varied and differ from one school to the next.

While there are several mitigating circumstances, most often they show up when the board lacks an understanding of how the evaluation process works. Dysfunctionality or simply immaturity on the board or a board that is simply dysfunctional can contribute to these mitigating circumstances. Unfortunately, with a few boards, arrogance leads to a poor evaluation process. This occurs when several board members believe that the head is an employee rather than a valued partner in the process. This usually reveals that the board is not functioning well in several areas, and often particularly in the area of appropriately evaluating the head. . . .

In many instances, a board's inability to fully understand the head's role is staggering. The board's expectations are often unrealistic with little basis in the history of the school or in the reality of current and future circumstances. For example, why would a board have as a goal raising an amount of money in two years when that amount had never before been raised in ten years? This is a clear case of a complete lack of collaboration between board and head.

Numerous questions surface as to why this is so:

- Why do boards continue to operate in this way?
- Why do heads allow such an environment to exist?
- Where are the enlightened board chairs and members that recognize this is not a healthy environment?
- Is there an evaluation model that, with certain modifications, is beneficial to most independent and faith-based schools?

The answers can often be found, as is often the case, in board education or training as well as a belief that best practices make a difference!

There are those who make the case that simply having an evaluation process is sufficient for a school. This is actually not true as many evaluations do significantly more harm than good. These lead to hurt feelings, lack of trust and respect, a misunderstanding of the head's role and the board's role, and an inability to comprehend that the head needs the support of the board.

There are two aspects vital to evaluating the head of school. One is the board's overall evaluation of its own work. The other is making sure the evaluation process has been researched and proven to be the best fit for the school, head, and board. There are several models that exist, and some are quite good, however, each board should incorporate best practices into the process based on unique circumstances.

From the board's evaluation of its own effectiveness found in chapter 17 and Appendix H, these are the questions that pertain to the how the board should view its connection to the head:

Head of School
The relationship between the head of school, the board chair, and the entire governing board is critical to the health and sustainability of the school. The key questions that support this relationship include:

- Does the board support the head and view his or her role as one of partnership and collaboration?
- Does the head establish annual goals and set goals that reflect the mission and vision of the school?
- Does the board have in place a fair and helpful way to evaluate the work of the head?
- Is the evaluation presented in a way that demonstrates respect for the work performed by the head and the staff?
- Does the board provide in the budget continuing education and professional development opportunities for the head?

These questions set the tone for a positive relationship to occur. The second aspect of the evaluation process is the criteria and the process used for the evaluation. Consider this brief narrative from the perspective of a head of school on establishing the manner in which the evaluation would happen:

When I was hired as head of school, I requested and was given the opportunity to draft my contract. Based on many years of experience as the head of school, I had seen too many poorly written contracts that were either overly long and complex (nineteen pages) or others that seemed to be little more than a way for the head to be set up for failure—unrealistic expectations based on nothing more than a wish list. I believed then as I do now that the contract and any instrument used to evaluate the head should be tied closely together. My contract is two pages.

The board chair allowed me to draft the contract and I asked that my evaluation be based on the elements of the contract—metrics both measurable and issues that related to enhancing the quality of the school. Therefore, most of my evaluation is determined by the following:

1. Performance related to meeting budget expectations.
2. Growth in enrollment.
3. Retention goals—we have a goal of 90%.
4. Annual fund giving—both the budgeted goal as well as how we do in exceeding the goal.
5. Debt reduction. We currently have a fundraising campaign to reduce our long-term debt.
6. Faculty retention. High turnover would be considered a negative as relationships between faculty, students, and parents are considered a fundamental pillar at our school.

The board chair convenes a meeting with the other board officers. They make a recommendation to the full board who makes a determination as to compensation, the amount of any bonus, and an additional amount that I can use however I wish. One practice I have used is to reward a select group of faculty and staff with a year-end bonus.

It is a simple, straight-forward process that is effective for our school and our circumstances. Throughout the year I meet with the chair. There are no surprises at the end of the year, and she would not tolerate from all trustees anything other than a professional process absent gossip, rumor, secret meetings, etc.

In looking at the fundamental criteria for an evaluation, these are the steps needed to achieve a fair and supportive process:

- The evaluation is a shared experience in which the head of school has input into the performance criteria on which the evaluation is based.
- The evaluation takes advantage of the significant elements that are included in the head's contract.
- In addition to connecting the contract to the evaluation, the head of school and the board chair agree upon goals for the year. These goals are reviewed throughout the year—not just at the time of the evaluation.
- The board of trustees institutes its unique methodology for evaluation. It may include the creation of the committee on the head.
- This committee may include the officers of the board or may develop a different committee makeup. It should always include the chair of the board.
- The committee on the head meets formally at the end of the year to review the goals on which the evaluation is based.

- The committee makes a recommendation to the full board and the board votes on the recommendation.
- The board chair, representing the committee, meets with the head of school to report on the decision of the board.
- The board chair meets with the head of school prior to the beginning of the fiscal/academic year and discusses goals for the coming year.

Many schools have a process for evaluating the head of school. Is it fair? Is it encouraging? Is it supportive? Does it relate back to points in the contract? Does it allow the head to have input? Do the chair and the head work together to resolve any issues? If the answer to each of these questions is "yes!" then the school is on the path to addressing this issue in a manner that would align with best practices. That should always be the standard to achieve.

CASE STORY #22
"Aren't You Here to Do What We Tell You?"

Woodcrest Academy had been experiencing growing pains but was beginning to thrive in part because it was located in a growing, vibrant community. For this school, which had been founded about twenty-five years earlier, the organizational chart was fairly typical in that the board of trustees had one employee, Sandra, the head of school. And like many boards it operated effectively much of the time, especially when there was no controversial issue to deal with.

However, one particular area that the board felt strongly about and made a major part of their responsibility was the academic program. While they respected Sandra in her role as head of school, the board was convinced it knew more about the curriculum than Sandra and the professional educators. For her part, Sandra was anxious to work with the board and did an adequate job of steering such discussions to keep the focus on the mission and the curriculum. The curriculum was a combination of an innovative yet practical approach based on the firm philosophical belief that teachers should modify their teaching methods in recognition of different students' learning styles represented in any given classroom. In addition, Sandra believed in experiential learning and involving the students in the community as much as possible.

Over the course of the summer as planning for the next year was taking place, Sandra introduced to the faculty and staff a new initiative that involved mandatory community service and made this one of the requirements for graduation. The idea was originally considered in a slightly different format in the school's strategic plan. Sandra was convinced that there was significant merit in the concept of giving back to the community, making a positive difference, and learning that leaders are here to serve. Additionally, the program was an outgrowth of what had already been taking place at Woodcrest for the past several years. The faculty agreed and endorsed the plan with great enthusiasm.

Because Sandra knew the board wanted, even insisted, to be made aware of every programmatic change and revision, she would bring the new community service initiative to the board for approval. Prior to the board meeting Sandra followed her usual practice of meeting with Cindy, the board chair. The purpose was to discuss the agenda and be sure Cindy was aware of anything that would be cause for trustee discussion. Cindy supported the idea of community service and the process that Sandra had initiated with the faculty as well as Sandra's plan and timeline to inform the board.

At the next monthly board meeting, the stage was set for a discussion of the new mandatory community service program. In both Sandra's and Cindy's minds, these monthly meetings were too often, but this time-table was a "sacred cow" they were not ready to do battle over yet. Change did not come easy to this board. Only recently the board had reluctantly changed from "directors" to "trustees"—also a difficult discussion and close final vote. As a part of the head of school report, Sandra shared her reasons for the move to the required community service program. She ended by stating that the program would be implemented with the beginning of the next school year and that significant communication would precede the implementation of the program.

At the conclusion of her remarks Randy, a new trustee with a son and daughter at the school, was clearly upset and began to argue against the program. He was opposed to the idea of what he perceived as a volunteer program becoming compulsory. He argued with a raised voice against making something mandatory that should be borne of interest and commitment. Sandra was taken aback and shared that perhaps Randy did not understand the intent of the program. While giving back to the community might be the natural consequence of someone's behavior, she genuinely believed that a more formal program with the ultimate goal of a student discovering his or her passion for service was the right approach. She gave numerous examples of excellent independent schools that had embarked on similar programs.

Randy was unmoved and continued his argument. He began to turn his outrage to the chair, Cindy, and insisted she intervene and take his side. Cindy was stunned by the turn of events and was not sure how much additional support Randy had from other board members. While she sided with Sandra, she was reluctant to say too much at that point. Finally, after continued heated disagreement between Randy and Sandra, Randy said, "Aren't you here to do what we tell you to do?" This statement sucked all the air out of the room. For a moment, there was silence. Cindy stepped in, tried to remain neutral, and stated that the program would be tabled until the next meeting. In the meantime, the board would meet in executive session to discuss what had just occurred.

The question that Randy posed had never been considered or articulated until that moment. To be certain, candid discussion and disagreement is a part of the process, and trusting relationships are built on such dialogue. But in this case, is this what being a trustee means? Partnership, collaboration, shared vision, and other similar characteristics should define the working relationship between the head of school, board chair, and board members. However, what happens when one or a few members of the board are firmly convinced that this relationship goes beyond the head's reporting to the board (and each trustee)? Should the head understand that he or she is required to do what the board wants—regardless of the situation or specific circumstances?

Questions for Discussion

1. *In what different way could Sandra have introduced the program?*
2. *What is the role of the chair in managing and mediating such a discussion?*
3. *What does this episode say about the culture of the board? Respect? Shared vision?*
4. *What do you think about one board member or a minority of trustees having the right to dictate an agenda?*
5. *Why wasn't this program simply reported as a matter of information?*
6. *What role does a perceived genuine difference make in the discussion?*
7. *What function does board selection and education have in this situation?*
8. *In what way do you believe Sandra's position is being threatened?*
9. *What should be the next steps for the Woodcrest board?*
10. *What would happen if this were to be discussed in executive session, without the presence of the head of school?*
11. *Is the head required to do what the board wants, or is there another way to move forward?*

Chapter Twenty-Four

◆

The Role of the Director of Advancement (Chief Development Officer)

It is universally agreed that the board of trustees has a direct role and responsibility to ensure the school has the resources necessary to not only sustain the school but position it in such a way that it thrives.

The director of advancement, or chief development officer, has a unique relationship with the governing board. Because both fundraising and the marketing of the school are critical to its ability and opportunity to fulfill its mission, the person in this role works closely with the entire board.

The titles and responsibilities of this office vary widely among independent and faith-based schools. Development goes under numerous names including:

- Resource Development
- Advancement

- External Affairs
- External Relations
- Fundraising

The responsibilities vary as well. For some independent schools, development may include not only fundraising functions but also alumni affairs, communications, marketing, and admissions/enrollment management. Depending on the size and structure of the school, they may lump development and fundraising along with marketing, communications, and any external relations functions—even though these activities and roles are quite unique—into a single office or even one individual.

For purposes of this chapter, the focus is on the person who is the individual who holds the responsibility for reporting directly to the head of school. As the director of advancement, this individual may work directly with the board of trustees in the following ways:

Serves as a liaison with the development committee of the board.

Working with the development committee of the board is near the top of the list of responsibilities for almost every director of development. This will include in conjunction with the committee chair, working on the agenda, preparing all materials for the committee's review, leading or participating in all committee discussions, attending all board meetings, and providing the committee chair with the data and information needed to give the committee report.

It is also critical that the director of development have the best possible relationship with the committee's chair. Depending on the school, this chair may change every year or two years requiring the development officer to work with or "train" someone with somewhat limited fundraising experience. Continuity is an important factor in success; however, this may be difficult to achieve.

One of the most important aspects of this relationship is the ability to equip the committee chair with the most effective way to communicate to the board the necessity of its role in giving and participating in the school's fundraising priorities. Establishing this as a priority will enable the board to set a more aggressive goal than 100 percent participation. Challenging the board in appropriate and meaningful ways will set the stage for more dynamic results.

Works with the head of school and development committee to formulate all aspects of the fundraising plan.

The director of development, or advancement, has an important relationship with the board's development committee. The director and the development committee provide strategic direction for the school's fundraising objectives. Fundraising plans typically fall under one of these categories:

- Major or capital gifts
- Annual fund
- Endowment and planned giving
- Special fundraising events
- Small capital or programmatic projects

The development committee is also charged with formulating the goal and plans to raise money from the board of trustees. The director of development works with the committee to ensure that there is 100 percent participation from the board.

The director of development, head of school, and the development committee will collaborate to set the annual fund goal and possibly other fundraising goals. The annual fund is particularly important in that there will be a line in the budget that corresponds to some or all of the total of the annual fund goal.

It is likely that the director of development will find it necessary to provide the strategic direction to the development committee that enables this group to carry out the task of soliciting the board in a way that will maximize results.

Works with the head of school and strategic planning committee to provide fundraising information for the strategic initiatives that require additional funding.

In other words, connecting the strategic plan with the most useful and effective mechanism to fund that portion of the plan. Often the strategic planning process does not actively engage the development leadership in considering existing funding opportunities and challenges that must be addressed as part of defining the strategic direction. Such an initiative without understanding revenue sources is not only inadequate but fails to uncover potential support.

Works with the head of school to create a plan that encourages all trustees to participate in professional development.

It's important to find learning opportunities for the board that are specifically related to its role in fundraising. This is also a place for the development committee chair to demonstrate leadership and "lead by example" by participating in professional development opportunities.

Develops the information utilized in the new trustee orientation program.

Along with the head of school and chair of the development committee, the director of advancement leads this portion of the orientation session. Ideally, fundraising was discussed as an expectation when the prospective trustee was recruited. If not, the orientation session must introduce this issue as a significant priority.

Works with the committee on trustees by identifying prospective trustees.

While it may be rare for the chief development officer to be included on the committee on trustees, there is good reason to have this person, along with the head, as an ex-officio member of this committee. These two individuals in these two incredibly important staff roles are in key positions to provide unique insight about prospective trustees being considered.

Clearly fundraising has been established as one of the more important factors when considering someone for the board. If this is true, then it follows the board would want the best information possible. The argument against this might be that the development officer could simply pass along names to the head for committee discussion. However, questions may surface in the meeting that the development officer is uniquely qualified to address, and his or her input and expertise could prove vital to the process.

* * *

What may be best for the school is to position the chief development officer as the number two staff person. Both perception and reality are part of this strategy. The board of trustees is going to recognize and realize that development, the fundraising and revenue-generating arm of the school, is placed directly behind the head. The chief development officer will be viewed as a leader worthy of all that goes with being one of the most valued members of the staff. Certainly there can be worthy discussions about placing other senior administrators in key roles. The director of enrollment management and marketing should be viewed as one such position.

The other central message has to do with sustainability. We live in challenging times in which there are many opportunities but also many threats to not just thriving, but surviving. Where the chief development officer is placed in the hierarchy says something about recognizing that sustainability is the inescapable reality for the school.

CASE STORY #23
Trusting the Process

It was just like clockwork. On the days the board's development committee met, the committee chair, Laura, always called the director of development, Tina, in the morning and the head of school, Tom, in the afternoon about an hour before the meeting began. One of the several interesting facets of these calls is that Laura never told Tina or Tom that she had called the other.

The school had an excellent track record in fundraising. The number of donors and the number of new contributors was growing every year since Tina and Tom's arrival. They made an excellent team and the results were amazing. The two leaders were trying to work with the development committee, but it was clear the committee had an agenda that questioned and second-guessed almost every decision. To the committee, the expectation was one of catch-up. The school had experienced a poor decade in which very little was accomplished in raising money. It was as if the development committee wanted to make up the difference in two years—an unrealistic expectation that demonstrated the committee's lack of understanding of the fundraising process.

Prior to each development committee meeting, Tina prepared the preliminary agenda, discussed it with Tom, and then sent it to Laura for her input once they felt good about it. More often than not, Laura would have little to say about the agenda. And then, the day of the meeting, the calls would begin. Laura would ask Tina more about fundraising "gossip" rather than a discussion regarding anything substantive. In addition she would ask Tina what Tom was doing—an indication that Laura thought he was probably not doing enough!

Then Laura would call Tom and ask the "how's everything going?" question—looking for any information that would suggest answers to "why aren't you doing more?" or "what are your impressions of Tina's performance?" Laura would never exactly phrase her questions or concerns in this way, but that was clearly the underlying message—I'm questioning you, and as a trustee ("your boss"), I have every right to do so.

Tina and Tom would compare notes and shake their heads about Laura. It was obviously important for this relationship to work—there was a lot at stake. However, neither Tina nor Tom knew how to move forward. They would ask:

- Why was she doing this?
- Does she not trust our work, dedication, and ability to get the job done?
- Was she purposefully trying to test what we said about one another?
- Does she not believe we talk with one another?
- Where is the trust between board member and staff?
- What are Laura and the development committee looking for that isn't being accomplished?
- Is there any evidence that suggested they we're not meeting goals and expectations?

These were all troubling questions. The two staff leaders were not sensing the support and encouragement so necessary to gain the most out of this relationship.

Questions for Discussion

1. *When Laura calls Tina and Tom separately before the meeting, what messages does she send about their relationship, about trust and collaboration?*

2. *Personalities and attitude play an important role in relationships. What can you glean from the personalities and attitudes of Laura, Tina, and Tom?*

3. *As the school's head, what should Tom communicate to the board chair regarding the way in which the development committee was operating?*

4. *How can the board chair address what is a delicate matter between two trustees?*

5. *Would it be appropriate to "confront" Laura and discuss the situation?*

6. *Should Tina and Tom simply wait until another committee chair is appointed?*

7. *Would Laura benefit from and be willing to participate in a professional development opportunity (seminar or workshop)?*

8. *When trust is not obvious, how can that be reclaimed?*

9. *How would you resolve this matter?*

Chapter Twenty-Five

◆

Creating and Sustaining the Advisory Board: Twelve Steps to a Meaningful Program

The decision to create an advisory board is one that should be made carefully with the understanding that creating such a board should be done with the belief that it will be viable for the long term. All too often schools will create an organization like this with no clear vision of its strategic significance. While there is no one correct way to establish such a board, it's creation should be done with the head's blessing, if not direction. In addition, the school's governing board of trustees should embrace the formation of the advisory board by recognizing the role it is intended to play.

To give the advisory board every chance for success, there are a number factors and steps that must be considered before the first person is invited onto the advisory board. While these steps do not guarantee long-term viability, the absence of this thoughtful approach may mean a quick exit for the advisory board. Adherence to the following steps will set the course for creating and sustaining the school's advisory board.

Step One: Establish Purpose and Mission

Establishing the scope and purpose of the advisory board includes the creation of a mission statement. While it may seem obvious, the determining factors must be considered prior to moving forward on any aspect of the creation of an advisory board. These factors are: What is the purpose of the advisory board? What is its goal and what mission statement will guide its actions? There is often the temptation to take a broad-brush stroke with this step, having only a vague idea of what the school is hoping to achieve. Do not fall prey to this temptation. The better strategy being specific as possible while at the same time allowing for some flexibility in the process. Having a mission and purpose does not mean adopting of something grandiose or wordy that is not practical and meaningful.

Will the board be involved with fundraising? Will it involve advice on certain aspects of the academic program, athletics, or arts? Will it be more general in nature, meaning that members could be asked for their advice or input on a range of topics? Will advice be sought on new initiatives that potentially impact many aspects of the school? Will it be project related, meaning that the advisory board will move from one project to the next?

Step Two: Define Roles and Responsibilities

Remember, this is not the governing board and therefore the roles and responsibilities should look very different. However, it is important as this will need to be communicated with prospective members of the advisory board. It should be made clear what their roles and responsibilities do *not* include. Typically, their responsibilities should not include hiring decisions, fiduciary matters, strategic planning, or fundraising responsibilities (unless this is one of the specific reasons the board has been created).

Listening is key. Never underestimate the power of the right group of people hearing the school's thoughts, ideas, and plans to sustain a meaningful, impactful future for the school. The result can be valuable input that can help shape the strategic thinking about what is the best and most appropriate way to move forward.

Some schools may choose to create an advisory board with very specific intentions because of certain gaps or needs that have been identified as priorities. Many schools find that they need assistance with fundraising and establish a board they believe can be an effective outlet for such work. Other schools use this board as a landing place for former trustees, honoring them for their faithful service and giving them the opportunity to make a difference through their knowledge, expertise, and community involvement.

One thing that is almost a certainty is that the advisory board will, or should, have some type of ambassadorial role. Independent and faith-based schools need advocates—champions who understand and are willing to communicate to the broader community what the school is about, what it is trying to accomplish, and the positive impact it has on students and the community. All too often the opinions of these schools are shaped by a misguided perception of being only for the affluent, elite, academically gifted, and that gifted athletes are provided "scholarships." Once this perception takes hold, it is hard to alter the way people think; the perception becomes the reality. Word-of-mouth marketing is a strategy that has taken hold because it has such an important impact on the school. Therefore, the more people connected with the school who are actively engaged in talking positively about the school, the better chance there is of ensuring a positive impression.

Step Three: Designate a Name

What's in a name? Choose wisely as the name of this board will go a long way in creating the most positive attitude or opinion about this new group. The appropriate name signals that there is clarity about this advisory board's intentions. Consider incorporating a name that reflects something unique about the school. Here are a few of the most commonly used names that indicate that the organization is intentionally a support organization and not a governing board:

- Board of Advisors
- Board of Associates
- Board of Visitors
- Advisory Council
- Leadership Council

Step Four: Establish Guidelines, Bylaws or None of the Above

Some level of validation for the advisory board helps to legitimize the work of this group. However, a certain amount of flexibility allows the school to make changes as needed. Then the question becomes, for the work of this organization, is it preferable to create guidelines or is there a need to provide a different level of formalization by creating bylaws?

Guidelines, as the name somewhat implies, are just that—a set of principles or ideas that provide general direction to the organization. Modifications are more easily made when the need arises to make certain changes. Flexibility is the key as is the ability to make changes on short notice without having to hold a meeting or take a vote. With guidelines, it is easier to adjust the number of meetings, members, even terms of office. And, the school can always shift from guidelines to bylaws.

Bylaws have much more of a tone of legalism and convey the perception that this is a formal organization, similar to the governing board, which is required to have bylaws. Some schools feel strongly that the organization is more legitimate if it operates under the watchful eye of a set of bylaws.

Then there are schools that choose to have neither guidelines nor bylaws but prefer a few simple thoughts written down that provide all the formalization needed for the organization to exist. It may be nothing more than a vague purpose for the organization, the name of the organization, how often meetings are held, and an approximate number of members. After that, they are off and running with the freedom to function in a manner that best suits their purposes.

The point is that the school work through these issues on the front end and be proactive in terms of creating the type of advisory board that is desired. Whether guidelines, bylaws, or nothing at all, the key is to make a commitment to creating something meaningful to those who are involved and those you want to be involved in the future.

Step Five: Determine the Appropriate Size

Size matters, and giving thought to this issue will determine how much input the school wants to have on any given idea or initiative.

Some schools have adopted the strategy that fewer in number means higher selectivity or a more exclusive group in terms of honoring or recognizing certain aspects of achievement. Other schools have taken on the philosophy of "The more, the merrier!" When it comes to meetings, it may be detrimental to have only a few, thus risking an even smaller number who may actually attend a meeting. This may be the place where the school begins to give serious thought to the structure of the meeting—is it meaningful, informative, interesting, interactive, and somewhat entertaining? If these elements do not exist, it will be difficult to convince these board members to return for the second meeting. Best to do some significant planning and prove to the organization's members that the school is prepared to make this a positive experience and one that they will look forward to attending again.

More often than not, the school will establish the advisory board to be a fundraising source—the members themselves as well as the access they might have on others. From the perspective of member recruitment, the school's approach may be telling prospective members that they are needed in considering a particular initiative or project that requires a certain level of capital funding beyond what is in the budget. From a purely fundraising standpoint, it makes the member feel special for his or her advice to be sought regarding plans the school has to enhance its future.

Size will also be a factor depending upon whether or not the school chooses to have standing committees or groups designated as committees centered around an event, project, or something that is ongoing or continuous in nature. It is a challenge to have several committees when there are only a few members to choose from. When you begin to have committees, the advisory board begins to look more like your board of trustees. Is that the goal? If so, that is great. Be sure that is an objective—more structure when creating the advisory board.

Another factor when determining size has to do with the school and the desire of the board of trustees to potentially recruit new trustees from this new board. Schools have effectively used this board as a "proving ground" to determine if there is a possibility for certain advisory board members to one day become effective trustees. It is a place where they can be seen in action so to speak. Do they attend meetings? Do they listen and are they engaged? Are they committed to enhancing the school? Do they listen or does it appear to be all about them? Do they have a positive attitude? Do they appear to have an agenda that seems counter to the direction of the school? All of these factors are signs or indicators as to their future value as members of the school's board of trustees.

Step Six: Begin with the Most Effective Structure

While it is true that the establishment of an advisory board can certainly evolve over time, best practices would suggest that starting with what the school believes is the most beneficial would be the way to proceed. This is another example of how strategic thinking on the front end pays dividends as the school moves forward with the new advisory board.

When thinking about structure, the head of school along with any others involved—advancement, communications, alumni, and development are each possible places for the logistics of the advisory board to fall—must decide the level of priority for this new advisory board and how much time to devote to it. This factor, perhaps above all others, will determine the kind of structure the head will want to put in place. The more time devoted to this board, the more detailed structure is possible.

There are a range of issues that must be taken into consideration. What is the desired outcome and what structure should be put in place to achieve that outcome? Considerations include:

- Size of board
- Committee structure
- Frequency of meetings
- Recruitment of new members
- Terms of office
- Officers or not

These considerations will be reviewed in subsequent steps.

Step Seven: Consider Term Limits

Consideration of term limits is most often thought of in the context of the board of trustees. That is what schools are most familiar with. It should not be significantly different with an advisory board. Think through the process of recruiting these board members. What are you going to communicate regarding term limits? When recruiting, this issue will come up.

For the governing boards at many independent and faith-based schools, a three-year term is the most common. Does this make sense for the advisory board? Would a longer term be beneficial—perhaps five years? If the structure of the advisory board is not too complex or too intrusive, then a prospect is more likely to agree to a longer term. A five-year term with two meetings each year is a term limit many will find acceptable.

Some advisory boards have no term limits. Others encourage but do not prescribe exactly what the expectations include. It is more of a recommendation making it easier for advisory board members to come and go as their schedules allow.

Step Eight: Choose Officers for the Advisory Board

Responsibilities, the scope of work, the complexity of the structure, and other factors will dictate the need to have officers. Perhaps all that is needed are a chair and a vice chair. Is a secretary or treasurer necessary? One important consideration is the relationship between the board of trustees and the advisory board. Some schools have made the decision that a representative from the advisory board will be an ex-officio member of the board of trustees. This means that the chair of the advisory board will, by virtue of that position, serve on the board of trustees without a vote. A typical scenario is for the chair of the advisory board to attend the board of trustees meeting, present a report of activities to the trustees, and then leave following his or her presentation. Therefore, it makes sense for the advisory board to have at least one officer for the organization.

Step Nine: Determine Appropriate Number of Meetings

This topic always makes for an interesting discussion when this is on the table for the board of trustees. It is the same here. What is of most value to the advisory board in terms of meeting the objectives of the school? This should be the determining factor when taking into consideration the number of meetings to hold each year. Many advisory boards have decided to adopt a different schedule than that of the board of trustees. The typical advisory board is meeting two to three times a year. Once you begin to go beyond that number, it really becomes a time commitment factor for the head and other members of his or her staff. In an effort to maximize longevity, keep the meetings fresh and worthwhile, and ensure board members remain engaged, it is probably advantageous that the school consider fewer meetings for its advisory board.

Step Ten: Choose which Constituencies to Include

Independent and faith-based schools have as a part of their community a number of constituencies that impact school climate and culture. These include faculty, staff, trustees, former trustees, parents, parents of alumni, grandparents, alumni, vendors, friends of the school, and the broader community. The questions become which constituencies to include, depending upon objectives, and which to exclude and why.

As stated in earlier steps, the objective of the advisory board has much to do with deciding which constituencies to include. Most advisory boards do not include faculty and staff because of their extensive engagement and time commitment with the school. Parents, grandparents, and alumni should all be considered. In addition, this may be an excellent opportunity to connect with the broader community—those who do not have a direct connection with the school. Independent and faith-based schools sometimes have a difficult time connecting with this constituency. However, if thoughtfully considered and coupled with a personal contact from the head of school, it could result in the beginning of a strong relationship. Perhaps here is where the mayor, city manager, or another government official could be a great choice. This also might be the place for representatives from the local chamber of commerce. The possibilities are numerous and, given the proper care in selecting individuals who you want to learn more about the school, could enhance the school in numerous ways.

Step Eleven: Establish Geographical Boundaries

Because advisory boards typically meet less frequently than other types of boards, this presents the school with the opportunity to create a board that does not have the same geographical limits as perhaps the governing board that may meet four to six times a year. This unique situation allows the head of school and others charged with putting together the advisory board to think regionally if not nationally. Independent school alumni are often scattered across the country if not the world. These individuals may be leaders in a variety of vocational capacities whose input on the advisory board could be enormously meaningful and insightful. Think of the unique perspective and skills such individuals could have. It is a powerful opportunity the school should consider.

Often schools do not have volunteer placements for parents, grandparents, parents of former students, alumni, and even former trustees. An advisory board may allow them to remain deeply engaged or honor their previous service to the school. An advisory board presents so many possibilities for creating, building, or rewarding relationships. And these relationships may prove to be vital in sustaining the school well into the future.

Step Twelve: Recognize the Advisory Board

It is almost never a bad idea to find ways to recognize and thank volunteer leaders for the work they do for independent and faith-based schools. It is, however, something of a challenge to do this in a way that is genuine and creative. Here are some ways that may work:

- List the members along with their picture (either individually or as a group) on the school's website with a brief explanation of their role in the school.
- Highlight members in the school newsletter.
- Recognize members at certain school events, such as one of the back-to-school activities. Find the right event and

audience to recognize the advisory board. Veterans Day or Grandparent Day events are prime examples.

- Ask members to speak at school events such as chapel services, school assembly programs, or speak to certain classes.
- Consider media releases when the advisory board is created. This announcement and other media releases are important. Find out where volunteers went to school and their home town and send an announcement to those places as well.

While advisory board members are not seeking recognition, it becomes the responsibility of the school to take this obligation seriously. It is good stewardship and, as a result, the advisory board member will feel proud to be a part of a school that means something to them and makes a difference in their community and beyond.

The twelve steps described here provide a road map for the school as way to extend its impact and footprint and engage with its immediate community as well as the broader community in powerful ways. While it may not be the path for every independent or faith-based school, every school should take a closer look and discover what is best. It may well mean that having some type of advisory organization can make a real difference. And that is what independent and faith-based schools should be about—making a positive difference.

* * *

NOTE: In reviewing these twelve steps to ensure creating and sustaining the advisory board for the school, it is fair to say that much of what has been communicated in these steps will also apply to establishing the governing board of trustees. It is worth examining this material from that perspective to determine if and how this information may be applied to the various criteria in establishing the board of trustees for the independent and faith-based school.

CASE STORY #24
Demonstrating Unwavering Support for the Head

For Marshall Academy, a lengthy search had resulted in the hiring of Martin to be its head of school. He was an experienced independent school leader, but he had never served as head before this appointment. Prior to his arrival, the board of trustees, along with the former head, had embarked on an extensive strategic planning process that called for numerous significant and far-reaching changes to the school. The board felt strongly that these changes were long overdue, and the new head and his staff would be responsible for implementing them. They were very much aware that some of the changes were controversial but made sure that Martin was aware of the plan prior to his appointment.

Martin's primary charge would be the successful implementation of the plan over the several years that had been outlined by the board of trustees. Martin arrived in July and immediately began his work of carrying out the directives identified in the plan. No sooner had Martin begun his work than the faculty became very upset with the plan and the manner in which Martin was attempting to implement it. They decided to take their case to the board and call for the head's resignation. Of course, Martin was stunned and deeply disappointed in how the faculty reacted. Why couldn't they see that the long-term benefits of the strategic plan would position Marshall for an exciting and rewarding future?

Faculty representatives petitioned the board to hear their concerns and made it clear they wished to see the new head fired immediately. The board listened to their points and afterward the chair of the board issued the following statement on the matter: *Upon further consideration, the board has elected to extend the head's contract for an additional five years.*

Questions for Discussion

1. *What does this story say about the relationship between the head and the board of trustees?*
2. *What could the faculty have done differently to share their concerns?*
3. *If you were the head of school, how would this statement make you feel?*
4. *How will the board's statement impact the relationship between the head and the faculty?*

Epilogue

◆

Independent and Faith-Based Schools Are Vital to Our Future

"Never underestimate the passion and commitment of a small group of dedicated individuals to change the world—indeed it is the only thing that ever has."

—*Margaret Mead*

Education is a vital component to our society and plays a prominent role in our nation's and, indeed, the world's future. For millions of students, education is the key to their success. Independent schools and faith-based schools are central to the way in which education is delivered. They have been a part of who we are as a nation from the very beginning, and they directly impact every facet of our lives. There are about fourteen thousand independent and faith-based schools in the

United States alone. And the common denominator for every one of these schools is that they all are required to have a governing board of trustees. These boards are made up of women and men who volunteer *their time, their talent,* and *their treasure*—an expression known to almost everyone who holds a leadership position in these schools.

The passion and commitment of those who work in the world of independent and faith-based schools is almost universal. These are individuals who desire to make a difference, to make a positive change in others, and to impact the lives of those they seek to influence. Why do we give a volunteer board of trustees the responsibility of developing the mission and vision of the school? It is a complex question. But since this is the case and it is unlikely this requirement will change, we must make every effort to ensure that each school's board has the very best volunteer board members possible to carry out their responsibilities.

The opportunities and challenges of maintaining, sustaining, and enhancing these schools are critical to the future of our society. We must be vigilant, and board and staff must work together to ensure that the days ahead are inspired and filled with opportunities to be a positive influence in this nation and around the world!

Through this book, I have attempted to convey how the governing board can transform independent schools and faith-based schools. Thoughtful, well-intentioned, engaged, and passionate leadership is required as this process unfolds to reveal the potential of the school. A clear and compelling vision combined with this model for leadership—both board and staff—is the "game changer." My hope is that some of this will resonate with you and that your board will become healthy, remain healthy, and ensure the brightest possible future for the students we educate.

Appendix A

◆

Suggested Topics
for Bylaws

The school's bylaws are required to be a legal, nonprofit organization recognized by the IRS with the 501(c)(3) designation that allows for tax-deductible contributions. The form, length, and wording vary from one school to another. Below are the basic topics that most schools should include in their bylaws.

1. Statement of purpose (the purpose, or mission, of the school must be articulated in the opening statements of the bylaws)
2. Powers or responsibilities of trustees
3. Description of circumstances that constitute voting membership
4. Tenure of service
5. Frequency of meetings
6. Number and description of standing committees

7. Description and responsibilities of the executive committee (if the board decides to have such a committee)
8. Election of officers
9. Powers and responsibilities of officers
10. Terms of officers
11. Appointment of committee chairs
12. Tenure of committees
13. Statement of fiscal year
14. Conflict of interest
15. Statement of nondiscrimination
16. Indemnification
17. Dismissal from the board
18. Dissolution statement

Appendix B

◆

Revising the School's Bylaws

The process of revising or, in some cases, rewriting the bylaws of an independent or faith-based school can vary from one school to another. It is critical that the school's head and board chair be in agreement regarding the need for revision as well as what specific changes are being considered. The process outlined below is one possible scenario that could be utilized:

1. The board chair and head agree on creating a bylaws committee with the specific charge of reviewing and revising the bylaws as may be needed.
2. This bylaws revision committee may include:
    *   Three members of the board
    *   The director of development
    *   Board chair
    *   Head of school
3. Determine which issues are to be addressed.

4. Consider having an objective perspective (consultant) to ensure that every issue is being considered. Having someone with experience and perspective could make a significant difference.
5. The consultant can incorporate revisions into the new draft of the bylaws.
6. Bylaws committee meets to work and make any necessary changes.
7. Changes are incorporated into a second draft for committee's consideration.
8. Final draft is prepared and sent to board.
9. Presentation is made to full board regarding revisions.
10. Board takes action on revised bylaws.

Appendix C

◆

Sample Bylaws

Name of School
BYLAWS

ARTICLE I
Name

The organization shall be known as [Name of School], hereinafter called [School].

ARTICLE II
Mission and Purpose

[School] is organized as a nonprofit, 501(c)(3) corporation, the mission of [School] is: A K–12 college preparatory school that creates programs and opportunities that inspire learning, advance knowledge, and build communities.

ARTICLE III
Board of Trustees

Section 1. Election. [School] shall designate a board of trustees who shall be elected by a majority vote of the members of the board, which shall occur, except in the case of filling vacancies, at each annual meeting.

Section 2. Number. The total number of trustees shall not be less than eleven (11) members, nor more than twenty-one (21) members.

Section 3. Term of Office. Each trustee will serve a term of three (3) years. Members may be nominated and elected for one (1) additional term of three (3) years. Members may not be elected beyond the second term unless they have been off of the board for a minimum of one (1) year.

Section 4. General Powers. The board of trustees shall have the general power and authority to manage and conduct the affairs of [School] and shall have full power, by majority vote, to adopt rules and regulations governing the action of the board of trustees.

ARTICLE IV
Meetings

Section 1. Regular Meetings. The board of trustees shall meet at least quarterly at a time and place designated by the board.

Section 2. Annual Meeting. One of the four (4) regular meetings shall be designated as the Annual Meeting. The purpose being the election of officers and the transaction of other business of [School].

Section 3. Special Meetings. Special meetings may be called by the chair of the board of trustees or a majority of the board. The person or persons authorized to call special meetings shall provide written or electronic notice of the time and location of the meeting and state the purpose thereof. No other matter shall be considered or discussed by the board of trustees at such special meeting except upon unanimous vote of the trustees present.

Section 4. Notice and Waiver. Notice of regular or special meetings of the board of trustees must be made in writing or in electronic form at least seven (7) days in advance of the meeting date. The attendance of a trustee at any meeting shall constitute a waiver of notice of such meeting.

Section 5. Quorum. A quorum shall consist of a majority of the trustees present at the meeting. If at any meeting less than a quorum is present, the majority may adjourn the meeting without further notice.

Section 6. Vacancy. Any vacancy occurring on the board of trustees shall be filled by a majority vote of the remaining trustees upon the recommendation of the committee on trustees. Each person so elected shall serve until the duration of the unexpired term. They shall be eligible for election for one (1) full term of three (3) years.

Section 7. Resignation. A trustee may resign from the board of trustees at any time by giving notice of resignation in writing, or e-mail addressed to the chair of the board.

Section 8. Removal. Any trustee may be removed by a majority vote of the remaining trustees at any meeting of the board of trustees. Such action may be the result of failure to act in the best interests of [School], failure to adhere to the principles described in the Covenant Agreement, or any other action which demonstrates a lack of support for the mission of [School].

ARTICLE V
Officers

Section 1. Designation of Officers. The officers of [School] shall be the chair, vice chair, secretary, and treasurer. The same person may hold no more than one office simultaneously.

Section 2. Election. The officers of [School] shall be elected at the designated annual meeting by a majority of the vote of the members of the board of trustees. Each officer shall be elected for a term of two (2) years. Officers may be elected for two (2) additional terms of two (2) years. No officer shall serve more than six consecutive years in the same office.

Section 3. Removal. Any officer may be removed by a majority vote of the board of trustees for failure to fulfill the duties as prescribed by these bylaws, conduct detrimental to [School], or for any other purpose judged not to be in keeping with the best interests of [School].

Section 4. Vacancy. A vacancy in any office for whatever reason may be filled by the board of trustees for the unexpired portion of the term.

Section 5. Chair. The chair of the board of trustees shall be the chief volunteer officer of [School]. The chair will lead the board of trustees in performing its duties and responsibilities. These shall include: presiding at all meetings of the board; serving as an ex-officio of all board committees; drafting and updating as necessary the Covenant Agreement; working in partnership with the head of school; and performing other duties as may be required by these bylaws and the board of trustees.

Section 6. Vice Chair. In the absence of the chair, for whatever reason, the vice chair shall perform all duties of the chair of the board. When so acting, the vice chair shall have all powers, responsibilities, and limitations of the chair. The vice chair shall have such other powers and responsibilities and perform such other duties prescribed by the board of trustees and the chair. Upon completion of the chair's term of office, the vice chair shall accede to the office of chair.

Section 7. Secretary. The secretary shall keep the minutes of the meetings of the board of trustees; ensure that all notices are duly given in accordance with the provisions of these bylaws or as required by law; and perform other such duties as from time to time may be assigned by the chair or by the board of trustees.

Section 8. Treasurer. The treasurer shall be responsible for all funds of [School]; receive and provide receipts for monies due and payable to [School]; deposit all such monies in the name of [School]; keep and maintain adequate and correct accounts; and render reports and accountings to the trustees. The treasurer shall also be the chair of the finance committee. The treasurer shall perform all duties incident to the office of treasurer and any other duties that may be required by these bylaws or prescribed by the board of trustees.

ARTICLE VI
Executive Committee

Section 1. The executive committee of the board of trustees shall consist of the officers of the board, the chairs of the standing committees, and one (1) at-large member of the board. The officers of the board shall be responsible for appointing this member.

Section 2. The chair of the board of trustees shall serve as the chair of the executive committee.

Section 3. The executive committee shall be delegated such powers and duties deemed advisable by the board of trustees, specifically including, but not limited to, the power to act on behalf of the board at such times when the board is not convened in regular or special meeting.

Section 4. The executive committee shall be responsible for setting the preliminary agenda for all board meetings.

Section 5. A majority of the executive committee shall constitute a quorum.

Note: More and more schools are deciding not to include the executive committee in their bylaws. There is the belief among these schools that the function of the executive committee no longer serves a meaningful purpose in the governance of the school.

ARTICLE VII
Committees

Section 1. Purpose. The board of trustees may establish standing committees to assist in the performance of its duties.

Section 2. Standing Committee. In addition to the executive committee, the other standing committees of the board of trustees shall include: the committee on trustees, the finance committee, and the development and marketing committee.

Section 3. Committee on Trustees. The committee on trustees shall be responsible for identifying, recruiting, training, and evaluating prospective and active trustees, consistent with the needs of [School]. The committee shall nominate trustees to serve as officers and members of the board. The committee shall also be responsible for the annual program of orientation of new board members and the ongoing education and evaluation of the board, including organizing and facilitating board retreats. The committee shall consist of no fewer than four (4) members of the board. The chair of the committee on trustees shall serve on the executive committee.

Section 4. Development and Marketing Committee. The development and marketing committee shall be responsible for ensuring that [School] maximizes its potential through fundraising efforts. In addition, the committee is responsible for [School] developing and maximizing a marketing strategy to ensure strategic potential is achieved. The chair of the development and marketing committee shall serve on the executive committee.

Section 5. Finance Committee. The finance committee shall be responsible for ensuring the financial sustainability of [School]. The finance committee prepares the preliminary budget and provides ongoing oversight of the budget during the fiscal year. In addition, the committee is responsible for supervising investments and ensuring the completion of the annual audit. The chair of the finance committee shall be the treasurer of the board of trustees and serve on the executive committee.

ARTICLE VIII
Conflict of Interest

The board of trustees affirms that the trustees, officers, administrators, faculty and other employees of [School] have an obligation to exercise their authority and to carry out the duties of their respective positions for the sole benefit of [School]. They should avoid placing themselves in positions in which their personal interests are, or may be, in conflict with the interests of [School]. Where a potential conflict of interest exists, it shall be the responsibility of the person involved or any other person with knowledge to notify the board of trustees of the circumstances resulting in the potential conflict so that the board of trustees can provide such guidance and take such action as it shall deem appropriate. Areas of potential conflict of interest are:

Section 1. Financial Interest. (A) Ownership by the individual directly or indirectly of a material financial interest in any business or firm (i) from which [School] obtains goods or services, or (ii) which is a competitor of the school. (B) Competition by the individual, directly or indirectly, with [School] in the purchase or sale of property or any property right or interest. (C) Representation of [School] by the individual in any transaction or activity in which the individual, directly or indirectly, has a material financial interest. (D) Any other circumstance in which the individual may profit, directly or indirectly, from any action or decision by [School] in which he or she participates or which he or she has knowledge of.

Section 2. Inside Information. Disclosure or use by the individual of confidential information about [School], its activities or intentions, for the personal profit or advantage of the individual or any person.

Section 3. Conflicting Interests Other than Financial. Representation as director, officer, agent, or fiduciary of another company, institution, agency, or person in any transaction or activity that involves [School] as an adverse party or with adverse interests.

Section 4. Gifts and Favors. Acceptance of gifts or favors from any firm or individual that does or seeks to do business with, or is a competitor of [School] under circumstances which imply reasonably that such action is intended to influence the individual in the performance of his or her duties.

No trustee who directly or indirectly is involved in a potential conflict of interest shall be counted in determining the existence of quorum at any meeting of the board where the potential conflict is considered, nor shall the trustee vote on any action of the board regarding that potential conflict.

ARTICLE IX
Statement of Nondiscrimination

[School] shall offer all programs and services without regard to race, color, creed, religion, or national ethnic origin, sex, or age and shall not discriminate on any of these bases in the administration of educational policies or admissions.

ARTICLE X
Parliamentary Authority

The rules contained in *Robert's Rules of Order*, latest edition, shall govern all meetings where they are not in conflict with the bylaws or other state laws pertaining to 501(c)(3) organizations.

ARTICLE XI
Indemnification

Unless otherwise prohibited by law, [School] shall indemnify any trustee or officer, any former trustee or officer, any person who may have served at its request as a trustee or officer of another corporation, whether for-profit or nonprofit, and may, by resolution of the board of trustees, indemnify any employee against any and all expenses and liabilities actually and necessarily incurred by him/her or imposed on him/her in connection with any claim, action, suit, or proceeding (whether actual or threatened, civil, criminal, administrative, or investigative, including appeals) to which s/he may be or is made a party by reason of being or having been such trustee, officer, or employee; subject to the limitation, however, that there shall be no indemnification in relation to matters as to which s/he shall be adjudged in such claim, action, suit, or proceeding to be guilty of a criminal offense or liable to [School] for damages arising out of his/her own negligence or misconduct in the performance of a duty to [School].

ARTICLE XII
Amendments

The bylaws may be altered, amended, or repealed and new bylaws adopted by a majority vote of the board of trustees present at any meeting. At least fifteen (15) days written or e-mail notice must be given of intention to alter, amend, or repeal the bylaws or to adopt new bylaws at such a meeting.

ARTICLE XIII
Dissolution

Upon dissolution of [School], the board of trustees shall, after paying or making provision for payment of all liabilities of [School], including expenses related to the dissolution, dispose of the assets of [School] exclusively for exempt purposes of [School] or distributed to another 501(c)(3) organization as determined by the board of trustees. None of the assets will be distributed to any officer or trustee of [School]. Any distribution of such assets will be done in a manner in keeping with the wishes of the state court having jurisdiction over the matter.

Appendix D

◆

Committee Job Descriptions

Included here are examples of job descriptions for two different standing committees found on many independent or faith-based school boards. While not necessarily required, such descriptions may be included in the school's bylaws.

Development Committee Description of Responsibilities

The development committee of the board:

1. Coordinates the fundraising activities of the school
2. Advises the board on the financial goals through the annual fund campaign, through the budget, and on any capital or endowment campaign
3. Supports the work of the development staff
4. Encourages *all* board members to be involved in development activities
5. Meets regularly to discuss issues and ideas that enhance the program

While the development committee has direct responsibility for the school's fundraising program, all board members must be informed and engaged in supporting the work of the committee as well as the development staff.

Strategic Planning Committee Description of Responsibilities

Working with the head of school, this committee coordinates the creation of the strategic plan, including mission, vision, goals, and objectives, with the support and approval of the board. The committee is responsible for monitoring the plan once it has been approved and adopted by the full board. As progress for achieving the goals of the plan may fall to different board committees, the strategic planning committee works closely with other board committees to ensure objectives are achieved. The development of action plans is the responsibility of the head and the school's staff unless the goal is a governance issue. The committee may include non-board members to address specific issues.

Appendix E

◆

Board Orientation
Sample Agenda

The board orientation session is critical to setting the expectations for each new board member. Coordination of the orientation is primarily the responsibility of the committee on trustees along with the board chair and head of school. Attendance is also required of all officers and standing committee chairs. Everyone on the board should be invited and encouraged to attend. Here is a sample agenda for an orientation session.

TOPIC	PRESENTER
Welcome by the head and the board chair	Head & board chair
Introduction of each new board member	Board chair
Brief history of the school	Head of school

Review materials included in board notebook*	Board chair & chair, committee on trustees
Review committee responsibilities	Individual committee chairs
Review financial position	Treasurer
Discussion and signing the Covenant Agreement	Board chair; chair, committee on trustees; head
Q&A	Everyone

*Notebook will include: bylaws, committee descriptions, minutes, listing of all trustees, listing of key staff, information related to the school, and any other information needed by the board.

Appendix F

◆

Board Retreat Sample Agenda

Under the guidance and leadership of the committee on trustees, the board chair, and the head of school, the board retreat is a significant opportunity to set the tone for addressing issues and challenges, recognition of expectations, and ensuring the adherence of best practices to secure a bright future. Also, the board may have completed a self-assessment questionnaire covering a range of topics.

The retreat may have different priorities and objectives—strategic planning, preparation for a campaign, or the introduction of some meaningful change being considered.

Here are the topics likely to be included:

- Introduction to the retreat and overview of the agenda
- Review self-assessment questionnaire
- Review planning process
- Discussion and review of the mission statement

- Discussion of opportunities and challenges (SWOT analysis)
- Planning components and critical issues prioritized
- Distinction made between short-term and long-range strategic goals
- Action plan and next steps determined
- Summary of plan and adjournment

Appendix G

$\blacklozenge$

The Covenant Agreement Sample

The strength of the school directly depends upon the willingness of the board of trustees to accept and carry out their leadership responsibilities to ensure that the mission and vision of the school is faithfully implemented. At the same time, the school has certain responsibilities to assist and support the board in its work. This Covenant Agreement is the document that sets forth these conditions as stated below.

Board of Trustees:

1. *I accept responsibility*, that as a member of the board of trustees, I have certain duties I must perform for the school to effectively and successfully function.
2. *I accept responsibility* for the future of the school. As a member of the board I pledge to understand and support the mission and vision of the school.

3. *I accept responsibility* to be knowledgeable of the school's bylaws.

4. *I accept responsibility* for securing understanding and acceptance of the school.

5. *I accept responsibility* to be knowledgeable of the school's operations, programs, and policies. I will be objective in my evaluation of the school.

6. *I accept responsibility* that while a member of this board I will make it a philanthropic priority to give to the school.

7. *I accept responsibility* to make financial contributions to the best of my ability. As a member of the board I will do all I can to ensure its financial well-being.

8. *I accept responsibility* to actively engage in fundraising activities on behalf of the school. This may include soliciting or contacting individuals, corporations, and foundations. It may also include volunteering to support school fundraising events. And it may also include acknowledging the support of contributors, and engaging in other fundraising activities necessary to advance the school.

9. *I accept responsibility* for the time commitment necessary to carry out the work of the board and the school. I understand this will include attendance and participation at board and committee meetings.

10. *I accept responsibility* in discharging specific duties that are assigned to me whether as a member of a committee or as a part of the general work of the board.

11. *I accept responsibility* to respect the work and authority of the board. I will be supportive of the decisions made by the board. If I am unable to accept the decisions of

the board, I understand this may mean stepping down or being removed from the board.

12. *I accept responsibility* for understanding and embracing the belief that conflicts of interest are unethical, are inappropriate, and undermine the work of the board and the future of the school.

13. *I accept responsibility* for respecting all opinions and discussions. I will not come to the board with a personal agenda nor will I impose my will to the detriment of the school.

14. *I accept responsibility* to abide by the principles articulated in the Governance Promise.

For the Covenant Agreement to be effective and meaningful, the school accepts responsibility to support the work of the board in the following ways:

School:

1. *The school* will provide to the board all documents and reports necessary for the board to function efficiently and effectively.

2. *The school* will make available any staff member necessary to discuss issues the board deems relevant and appropriate to its work. This may include staff and trustees working together on board committees.

3. *The school* will make every effort to be responsive to any questions that the board believes are necessary to carry out its responsibilities to the school.

4. *The school* will, along with the board of trustees, abide by the principles articulated in the Governance Promise.

Signed:

_____   _____
Member of the Board of Trustees   Date

_____   _____
Board Chair   Date

_____   _____
Head of School   Date

Note: While this document is not considered legally binding, it is essential that the board and the school recognize that these statements should guide and inform their work together.

Appendix H

◆

Evaluating the Board: Key Questions to Help Boards Sustain Excellence

A s the subject of chapter 4, the following areas of self-evaluation instrument will help create the framework to provide the data and information necessary for a board to sustain excellence. Take time now to work through this exercise.

Planning

The board should, almost above any other factor, be a group that devotes significant time to planning. The central questions in this area should include:

1. Is there a clear, succinct mission statement that is not only current but also understood by all trustees?
   ❑ YES
   ❑ NO

What will it take to move to (or stay at) YES?

_____

_____

_____

2. Is there a strategic plan, and is there a process in place for periodic review of the plan?
   ❑ YES
   ❑ NO

   What will it take to move to (or stay at) YES?

   _____

   _____

   _____

3. Have all facets of the school been considered when formulating the plan?
   ❑ YES
   ❑ NO

   What will it take to move to (or stay at) YES?

   _____

   _____

   _____

4. Do "action items" include a funding mechanism? Is there a way to fund the vision?
   ❑ YES
   ❑ NO

   What will it take to move to (or stay at) YES?

   _____

_____

_____

5. Does the board establish annual goals for itself?
   - ❏ YES
   - ❏ NO

   What will it take to move to (or stay at) YES?

   _____

   _____

   _____

6. Do board members participate in professional development opportunities?
   - ❏ YES
   - ❏ NO

   What will it take to move to (or stay at) YES?

   _____

   _____

   _____

Selection and Composition

There is nothing more critical to the success of a school than the processes in place for the selection and composition of the board. Answer these key questions, elaborating as much as possible:

1. What is the structure of the committee on trustees?

   _____

   _____

   _____

2. Is the committee active and engaged with all board members?

❑ YES

❑ NO

What will it take to move to (or stay at) YES?

_____

_____

_____

3. Does the committee have a matrix of prospective board members that identifies skills needed—both short-term and long-term?

❑ YES

❑ NO

What will it take to move to (or stay at) YES?

_____

_____

_____

4. Is the size of the board a positive or a negative?

❑ POSITIVE

❑ NEGATIVE

What will it take to move to (or stay at) POSITIVE?

_____

_____

_____

5. Are all committees functioning and effective?
   - ❑ YES
   - ❑ NO

   What will it take to move to (or stay at) YES?

   _____

   _____

   _____

6. Are the head of school and board chair included as ex-officio members of the committee?
   - ❑ YES
   - ❑ NO

   What will it take to move to (or stay at) YES?

   _____

   _____

   _____

Organization/Structure

How the board is organized reflects effectiveness in meeting the goals and objectives of the school. The key questions include:

1. Are the bylaws clear, concise, up to date, and followed?
   - ❑ YES
   - ❑ NO

   What will it take to move to (or stay at) YES?

   _____

   _____

   _____

2. Is the committee structure of the board valuable in meeting the demands of the board and the needs of the school?

    ❑ YES
    ❑ NO

    What will it take to move to (or stay at) YES?

    _____

    _____

    _____

3. Does the board seek ways to involve all constituencies of the school?

    ❑ YES
    ❑ NO

    What will it take to move to (or stay at) YES?

    _____

    _____

    _____

4. Does the board recognize and act on the difference between their responsibilities and those of the school's administration?

    ❑ YES
    ❑ NO

    What will it take to move to (or stay at) YES?

    _____

    _____

    _____

5. Overall, does the board understand its responsibilities?
   ❑ YES
   ❑ NO

   What will it take to move to (or stay at) YES?

   _____

   _____

   _____

6. Are there individual trustees who you believe may not be effective in their role?
   ❑ YES
   ❑ NO

   What will it take to increase his or her effectiveness?

   _____

   _____

   _____

7. Does the board review its work and is this process meaningful?
   ❑ YES
   ❑ NO

   What will it take to move to (or stay at) YES?

   _____

   _____

   _____

Orientation and Training

Orientation as well as ongoing training and education will encourage trustees to focus on being engaged in best practices. The key questions in this category include:

1. Is there a formal orientation session (including mentoring) for all new trustees?

   ❑ YES

   ❑ NO

   What will it take to move to (or stay at) YES?

   _____

   _____

   _____

2. Is there a board policy manual and does it include information useful to becoming familiar with the work of the board and the school?

   ❑ YES

   ❑ NO

   What will it take to move to (or stay at) YES?

   _____

   _____

   _____

3. Does the policy manual include a clear definition of conflict of interest and how the board addresses this issue?

   ❑ YES

   ❑ NO

What will it take to move to (or stay at) YES?

_____

_____

_____

4. Is there a structured, formalized program for board education?
   ❑ YES
   ❑ NO

   What will it take to move to (or stay at) YES?

   _____

   _____

   _____

5. Is funding available for board members to attend/participate in professional development opportunities designed for the board?
   ❑ YES
   ❑ NO

   What will it take to move to (or stay at) YES?

   _____

   _____

   _____

6. Does the board conduct an annual or periodic retreat as a way to explore a range of issues beneficial to both the board and the school?
   ❑ YES
   ❑ NO

What will it take to move to (or stay at) YES?

_____

_____

_____

Meetings

Meetings set the tone for a "board culture" that in many ways defines who board members are, how they operate, and what impact they have. Questions regarding frequency and length should be considered important to the effectiveness of the board:

1. Is the current number of meetings per year about right? Are more needed and why? Are fewer needed and why?

   _____

   _____

   _____

2. Do board meetings typically last longer than two hours?
   ❏ YES
   ❏ NO

   Why is this length too long, too short, or just right?

   _____

   _____

   _____

3. Is the agenda properly prepared and reviewed by the chair of the board or executive committee prior to the meeting?
   ❏ YES
   ❏ NO

What will it take to move to (or stay at) YES?

_____

_____

_____

4. Are the agenda and supporting documentation sent to board members prior to the board meeting?
   ❑ YES
   ❑ NO

   What will it take to move to (or stay at) YES?

_____

_____

_____

5. Do committees meet at intervals between board meetings?
   ❑ YES
   ❑ NO

   What will it take to move to (or stay at) YES?

_____

_____

_____

6. Is the staff liaison role understood and respected by board committees?
   ❑ YES
   ❑ NO

   What will it take to move to (or stay at) YES?

_____

_____

_____

7. Are committee reports effective and useful?

❑ YES

❑ NO

What will it take to move to (or stay at) YES?

_____

_____

_____

8. Is financial information presented and conveyed in a manner that non-financial board members can easily understand?

❑ YES

❑ NO

What will it take to move to (or stay at) YES?

_____

_____

_____

Individual Trustees

Because each trustee is a key member of the board, the manner in which each trustee does his or her job is essential. The key questions for specific trustees are:

1. Does each board member seem to be prepared for both committee and board meetings?

❑ YES

❑ NO

What will it take to move to (or stay at) YES?

_____

_____

_____

2. Do you believe each member capably performs both as-
   signed and volunteered responsibilities?
   ❑ YES
   ❑ NO

   What will it take to move to (or stay at) YES?

   _____

   _____

   _____

3. Are board members encouraged to recommend others to
   serve on the board?
   ❑ YES
   ❑ NO

   What will it take to move to (or stay at) YES?

   _____

   _____

   _____

4. Do you believe board members make giving to the
   school a priority?
   ❑ YES
   ❑ NO

   What will it take to move to (or stay at) YES?

   _____

_____

_____

5. Do board members recommend donors and solicit support?
   ❑ YES
   ❑ NO

   What will it take to move to (or stay at) YES?

_____

_____

_____

Head of School

The relationship between the head, the board chair, and the entire governing board is critical to the health and sustainability of the school. The key questions that support this relationship include:

1. Does the board support the head and view his or her role as one of partnership and collaboration?
   ❑ YES
   ❑ NO

   What will it take to move to (or stay at) YES?

_____

_____

_____

2. Does the head establish annual goals and set goals that reflect the mission and vision of the school?
   ❑ YES
   ❑ NO

What will it take to move to (or stay at) YES?

_____

_____

_____

3. Does the board have in place a fair and helpful way to evaluate the work of the head?
   ❑ YES
   ❑ NO

   What will it take to move to (or stay at) YES?

   _____

   _____

   _____

4. Is the evaluation presented in a way that demonstrates respect for the work performed by the head?
   ❑ YES
   ❑ NO

   What will it take to move to (or stay at) YES?

   _____

   _____

   _____

5. Does the board provide in the budget continuing education and professional development opportunities for the head?
   ❑ YES
   ❑ NO

   What will it take to move to (or stay at) YES?

   _____

   _____

   _____

Appendix I

◆

Ten Board Best Practice Issues That Impact Your School

While there are many influences and influencers mentioned in my previous book, *The Board Game*, there are ten that rise to a particular level and can be identified as those that are the most impactful and meaningful to independent and faith-based schools.

NUMBER TEN
Attitude is Everything

"Nothing can stop someone with the right mental attitude from achieving their goal; nothing on earth can help
someone with the wrong mental attitude."
—*Thomas Jefferson*

A positive attitude is essential. If you don't think so wait until
you encounter someone with a really bad one and then try to
work together to achieve certain goals. A person's outlook, or
view of the world, has so much to do with how well he or she
will relate to others. Do members of your board have a positive
attitude? Are they team players with the kind of can-do attitude
that inspires and encourages others? Do they value working
together and recognize that consensus and team-building foster
commitment to the school as opposed to focusing on self-interest?

Whether a board member or school leader, attitude will
define the school in important ways and serves as a revealing
expectation of what "being your best by doing your best" really
means. Board members should be leaders—and leaders are those
who inspire and encourage, individuals who set an example of
what is possible.

The key in having board members who exhibit a positive
attitude is to *recruit* them. The committee on trustees is charged
with identifying prospective trustees. One of the most important
characteristics that this committee should consider is attracting
someone who possesses a positive attitude!

NUMBER NINE
Finding Balance from the Board

"If we are together nothing is impossible, if we are divided all will fail."
—*Sir Winston Churchill*

Both the board chair and all trustees must avoid whatever *extremes* they bring to the boardroom. Discovering common ground and ways of working together for the good of the school adds both strength and sustainability. The value of teamwork is enormously important.

Every trustee comes to the board with strengths and weaknesses, likes and dislikes, and expertise and experiences. Much of this is valuable and certainly some of it is what attracted prospective board candidates in the first place. Having said that, board members may also arrive on the scene with strongly held opinions—perhaps too strongly held opinions. These opinions, whether professional or personal, can spill over into their board role and become unwarranted agendas. The agendas may replace what is best for the school. In these situations trustees have gone too far trying to force others to consider personal perspectives as school priorities.

There are many examples where strengths taken too far become detrimental. In this scenario the person comes on the board because of a particular knowledge of all matters financial. He or she has extreme views regarding cost controls, curtailing expenses, and making cuts as a way to advance the school. When these attitudes come into conflict with school priorities and different points of view held by a majority of the trustees, then the trustee must step back and accept that the board must speak with one voice.

Finding balance is the most effective way to govern. Trustees should monitor their behavior and when this does not seem to be working, the board chair must step in and provide the leadership and perspective to remind the board "team" that what is best for the school is what is best.

NUMBER EIGHT
Board Members with an Agenda

"All cruel people describe themselves as paragons of
frankness."
—*Tennessee Williams*

Even the best boards are subjected to chaos and often the reasons
center around those members who have an agenda. These board
members see the school from their own unique perspective,
unconcerned with whether or not their view might be harmful
and a distraction from the strategic direction of the school.

It is always fascinating when a school becomes completely
sidetracked by someone on the board who wants to hijack not
only board meetings but also the school to fulfill their wishes
and desires. And, what is more amazing is the number of schools
that succumb to this agenda time and again. To be sure many
individuals come to the board with certain beliefs and passions
about what they consider to be most needed. This is a good thing!
However, it becomes bad when it is your overwhelming reason
for being on the board—even when you recognize it is not a part
of the strategic direction for the school. Board members need to
be encouraged to remember it's not about them; it is about what
is the best strategy to move the school forward.

The wealthy and powerful are seldom told they are wrong.
This sometimes leads to bullying the other board members into
their way of thinking.

Why does this happen and why does the board allow this
to happen? Why is this someone we want on our board? More
often than not, the board knows this person and their MO. Do
they believe they can change them? Get them to give to areas that
most need support? It is rare that a "board bully" will change

his or her stripes. In the end the board bully is a huge distraction for the board, for the head of school, and for the school itself—consuming enormous amounts of time and energy dealing with what this trustee wants and must have!

What is the best way to have the kind of board members who will come to serve and act in the best interest of the school? The answer can be found in the process of board recruitment and how the committee on trustees carries out their work. This requires an investment in time that far too many schools don't wish to pursue. These schools miss the point that there is a direct correlation between the time invested in recruitment and the quality of the board member attracted to the school. What should be the composition of the committee on trustees? The overall size of the board will help dictate this. But ideally the committee on trustees should include three or four members of the board of trustees, the chair of the board, and the head of school. Including the board chair and head is essential to the process and these two may, if they believe it necessary, recommend that a particular individual not serve as a trustee. This type of relationship with an extremely important committee requires communication, trust, respect, collaboration and genuine leadership.

Someone with an agenda and resources may, at first, seem to be harmless—even helpful. But in the long run this agenda is more likely to be a distraction and destructive to the school.

William R. Mott, Ph.D.

NUMBER SEVEN
The Value of Consensus and Teamwork

> "We have committed the Golden Rule to memory; let us now commit it to life."
> —*Edwin Markham*

The issue of how a board of trustees carries out its work is one that impacts the school in significant ways. The principles of teamwork, trust, and partnership are central ones. Developing this list of ten reasons why consensus and teamwork is a productive way in which to resolve issues may be helpful. Being intentional and working together in a positive and productive manner will help focus attention on the strategic work of the board. Perhaps this list will generate healthy conversation among your board.

Ten Reasons to Embrace Consensus as the Way to Address and Resolve Board Issues

Many of the decisions made by trustees are made by consensus. Why is this the case and why is this the most effective way to lead and govern?

1. Define what consensus is and what it is not. Consensus has to do with the general agreement on a particular issue. It should not imply that the agreement has been reached without discussion.
2. The value of <u>consensus</u> is that it amplifies the most important characteristics that define the head and board relationship: communication and collaboration. Are we working together for common goals and to ensure the viability of the school?
3. <u>Consensus</u> builds support among board members. The opportunity to encourage open discussion on a particular topic

has the effect of building enthusiasm and a more positive response.

4. Think advisory. While a board certainly has fiduciary responsibilities for the school, many discussions and decisions are more advisory in their nature and impact. Providing advice and counsel and reaching a decision by consensus may be more helpful than needing to take a formal vote.

5. Consensus is another way to describe teamwork. When the board and head are "on the same page" there is a sense of shared vision and common purpose, a "pulling together" in a direction that is positive and productive.

6. Treating one another with respect will result in working together, and working together will result in building a stronger school.

7. Working toward consensus may reflect compromise but does so in the best sense of the word.

8. It's not all about you. While individual board members believe they have a compelling agenda, the ability to listen to other perspectives demonstrates a willingness to believe other ideas may be just as valid as yours.

9. There is strength in the concept of servant leadership. Leading by serving suggests a school that values putting the school above self.

10. The Golden Rule is golden for a reason. Our objective should be to treat others as we would like to be treated—and work with others as we would like them to work with us!

NUMBER SIX
The Board Leadership Transition

"Leadership and learning are indispensable to each other."
—*John F. Kennedy*

"Rough waters are truer tests of leadership. In calm water every ship has a good captain."
—*Swedish proverb*

Anytime there is a transition in board leadership for an independent or faith-based school, there is a risk that the leadership will not be as dynamic, not as effective as before. Of course there is the possibility that the incoming leadership will be stronger and even better than anticipated. Regardless, this transition from one board chair to the next may create some anxiety for the board and school. Ideally, this transition should be a smooth, seamless one, and not necessarily noticeable to the school's constituents.

One of the best ways to ensure the smooth transition in leadership is for this to be specifically included in the school's bylaws. Is there a provision for the vice chair to become the chair-elect? This is an important first step because it confirms that the vice chair knows when he or she is selected that the "grooming" has begun, which will eventually lead him or her to becoming chair of the board. Prior to someone being identified as a future vice chair (and, therefore, a future chair), the committee on trustees and the head should be completely involved in this discussion and selection. Their participation in this process is fundamentally important and a crucial factor in making the transition work.

The committee on trustees, the entire board of trustees, and the school's head must collaborate and communicate to make certain that whoever is selected as the vice chair/chair elect, that person brings to the position the balance to recognize the various contributions and schools of thought represented by the personalities found on the board. Compromise, consensus, and teamwork are key factors to making the transition harmonious.

NUMBER FIVE
The School's Governing Board Has One Employee

"A basic tenet of governance is that the board hires the
head who in turn hires all other staff."
—*From* The Nonprofit Secret *by Jonathan Schick*

Most everyone in the independent and faith-based school world
understands one of the most basic truisms that ensure these
schools possess the structure to succeed: the board of trustees
has only one employee, and that person is the head of school. It
follows then that every member of the school's staff, including
volunteers, in some way ultimately reports to the head.

Much more than anyone would care to imagine, board members
do not grasp this fundamental principle. There are numerous
reasons for this, including a lack of training and education, poor
attitude, and simply a belief that some rules don't really apply to
them. The result is that trustees will infuse themselves into the day-
to-day operational issues that are specifically not their responsibility
nor jurisdiction. Certain trustees are unable to distinguish between
what is operational and what is strategic, planning, policy, and
mission. Ultimately the board's role is viability—ensuring that the
school's future is secure, relevant, and sustainable.

This becomes a complex problem where trustees don't
realize that they are meddling and micromanaging. Tragically,
this behavior will often lead to intimidation and bullying. In
addition, trustees may also believe they have unfettered access to
anyone and everyone in the school, believing that "because I am
trustee, you must do as I say." If the school finds itself with this
kind of individual on its board, it becomes the responsibility of
the board's leadership—either the board chair or the executive
committee—to directly address this matter with the trustee. Some

who read this will shake their heads and say, "We have no such trustee." Congratulations! However, it is a short trip from not having someone who fails to get it, to having exactly this kind of person. Once again, it is in the recruitment of trustees where this issue can be raised relative to setting expectations.

Another reason this behavior exists can be found in various school constituencies who believe that the board should know everything going on in the school. The reality is actually quite different. There are numerous personnel issues, for example, when it is not appropriate and in fact not legal for the trustees to know. Yet many ask the question, "As a member of the board, aren't you supposed to know everything going on?" Parents often raise this question when a decision is made that they don't agree with. The issue is the board members must be educated on how to respond when that question is raised.

The most successful strategy to avoid this nightmarish behavior is to not tolerate it in the first place. This suggests that the responsibility for making sure this behavior does not occur falls to the committee on trustees and their role in making the effort to find the most "mission-appropriate" trustee possible. This is a person who understands, respects, and agrees to the information shared regarding what it means to be a board member. Perhaps the first issue that should be shared with prospective trustees is that the board of trustees has one employee.

NUMBER FOUR
Fundraising is Fundamental

"You make a living by what you get. You make a life by
what you give."
—*Sir Winston Churchill*

"In good times and bad,
we know that people give because you meet needs, not
because you have needs."
—*Kay Sprinkel Grace*

"For everyone to whom much is given, from him much
will be required."
—*Luke 12:48* NKJV

What is universally true about independent and faith-based
schools is that they each require financial resources (revenue)
to sustain their operation, provide capital for major projects,
and grow a healthy endowment ensuring sustainability for an
uncertain future. While there are no guarantees, what we are
objectively clear about is that these components are needed for
a school to contribute something significant to its students, our
culture, and society. If it is true that those closest to the school are
best suited to be its biggest supporters, then it stands to reason
that the board of trustees, collectively and individually, is in the
best position to provide this necessary financial support.

When a prospective trustee is recruited there are many issues
that must be discussed, including the issue that fundraising is
fundamental at a very personal level—meaning trustees must lead
by example when it comes to giving! Board members potentially
bring many needed attributes to their service on the board and

chief among these is the responsibility to give as generously as one is able to do. The committee on trustees (when recruiting), and the board chair, specifically, has the responsibility of candor. It may also fall to the board's development committee to make certain that 100 percent of the board members contribute. Nothing less is acceptable. There can be no disguising the fact that giving generously and supporting this process is the responsibility of each trustee. It may not be *the* reason someone was asked to join the board, but it is most certainly *a* reason. Never lose sight of the fact that for the board of trustees, *fundraising is fundamental!*

NUMBER THREE
Evaluation Is the Key to Understanding Where You Have Been and Where You Are Headed

Exhibit H

"The past is prologue."
—*From* The Tempest *by William Shakespeare*

Does past performance determine or influence future activities? Maybe. The question might be: Do you want to improve because you have not achieved to your capability? For the board of trustees the issue is: Can we be better, and how do we make this happen? Part of that answer may be found in whether or not the board evaluates its own work with the objective being improvement of their performance—not the performance of the head! That is an altogether different issue.

The board has an almost stated responsibility to demonstrate its leadership by evaluating the head. Using specific agreed upon criteria, the board measures the head's job execution and communicates strengths as well as areas of concern. To maximize their own work, the board should look inward to determine its strengths and areas of concern with the objective of aspiring to be a dynamic, thriving board that is always evolving to be the best possible. There are three different ways in which to assess how well board members adhere to these responsibilities.

The first is whether or not they have adopted the Governance Promise (chapter 20) as the way in which they govern their behavior, attitude, and their actions.

The second assessment mechanism is adherence to the Covenant Agreement (chapter 21, Appendix G)—a document they have signed stating that they will uphold very specific responsibilities and respect both the work of the board and the school.

The third way in which the board can review its work is the evaluation instrument and questionnaire found in chapter 17 and Appendix H. This resource breaks down board performance and responsibilities into seven different categories with questions in each category designed to pinpoint areas where the board is fulfilling its responsibilities, areas where they are not, and areas that require additional work.

The elements found in these three different but connected board resources will help measure meaningful value and are, in every way, a key to realizing a bright future. To get somewhere as opposed to anywhere, a strategy and a way to measure the results of that strategy are essential to realizing potential.

NUMBER TWO
The Board Chair and the Head of School Must Connect

"The best leader is one who has sense enough to pick good people to do what he wants done, and self-restraint enough to keep from meddling with them while they do it."
—*Theodore Roosevelt*

"If your actions inspire others to dream more, learn more, do more and become more, you are a leader."
—*John Quincy Adams*

Of all the issues that constitute an independent or faith-based school the most important is the relationship between the head and the board chair and governing board. This connection, this partnership will determine the school's success and vitality. If this relationship is working well then the school can truly focus on mission and vision. If this relationship is not working, though, the focus becomes: What's wrong? How do we make it right? Where do we go to get the professional assistance we need?

To truly understand the underlying issues that bring clarity to this challenge, one must return to those seven fundamental characteristics that define what makes it work:

1. *Collaboration and Communication*: Working together and having regular, ongoing communication is foundational for the relationship to be the best possible.
2. *Respect*: It is extremely difficult to work alongside and communicate with someone whom you do not respect or believe possesses the character and integrity that is an absolute requirement.

3. *Trust*: If there is respect, trust soon follows. The ability to believe in what each other is sharing carries with it enormous importance.

4. **Support**: What is all too often absent is a board chair who supports the head—especially when other board members are attempting to interfere with this leader's ability to manage the school. Knowing you have the support of the board chair brings confidence to do what needs to be done.

5. *Shared Vision*: When the board chair and head are "on the same page" with regard to the future of the school, it suggests a school that is thriving and meeting the needs articulated in its mission statement.

6. *Attitude*: People who are positive—who see the world in an optimistic way and who recognize they are blessed and in a position to share that outlook with others—are in the best possible position to influence the school in dynamic ways.

7. *Leadership*: The ability and opportunity to encourage, to inspire, and to bring out the best in others is a vital character trait. Can you, at the same time, be strong, kind, bold, thoughtful, humble, proud, and have a sense of humor? Then you might just be a leader.

8. Self-Awareness

NUMBER ONE
Partnership Is More Important than Hierarchy
(What's on the Organizational Chart)

"Never impose on others
what you would not choose for yourself."
— *Confucius*

"Teamwork is the ability to work together toward a
common vision. The ability to direct individual accomplishment toward organizational objectives."
—*Andrew Carnegie*

Working together to achieve mission and vision trumps any other way to accomplish the same thing. Independent and faith-based schools are essential to the very fabric of this country and too important to allow the intrusion of politics, personal agendas, poor attitudes, and other issues to hurt any school. And yet this happens because human nature kicks in and we allow, are unaware of, or even encourage individuals who possess these less-than-stellar traits to be on our boards. Of course, none of these individuals would recognize any failure on their part to be the best trustee. Just ask any one of them!

In a 501(c)(3) school, a governing board is required, and has the legal and fiduciary responsibility for sustaining the school. Board members "hold in trust" the school and, therefore, are at the top of the organizational chart. The head reports to the board. This has worked well for years, and many schools thrive in this structure and environment.

But how do we get from good to great in this hierarchal reality? What is really at stake? Is working together more important, more valuable than working in a "who works for whom" mentality? The answers can be found in genuine partnership—genuine teamwork. It is a recognition that working together is the value-added benefit that is truly at the heart of servant leadership and what makes independent schools unique in our culture. It is this unique characteristic that acknowledges, *It's not all about me!* Is there a time and place for this hierarchy? Absolutely. There are certain circumstances that dictate a chain of command and a "buck stops here" leadership style.

The example of vision, or strategic planning, provides a peek into what genuine partnership can look like. Often several school constituencies are involved with the board, having ultimate responsibility for the direction of the school. Why not include the head and senior staff in partnering with the board to determine the path ahead—by not just providing input but by acknowledging the special gifts each person brings to the enterprise? There are people with significant skills who contribute something profound to the conversation, but outcomes are diminished if those individuals are not included. Board members should embrace this.

Embedded in all of this is the almost lost art of listening and an attitude of gratitude! We are so often hung up on our position in the school (or on the board) that we forget the best strategy may be to sit down, be quiet, and listen to other perspectives. It is a hard lesson for all of us. This is not to imply that your opinion doesn't matter—it does. However, we too often believe nothing is more important than what we know and what we convey. As a result, we continue to miss opportunities to express appreciation for good work, acknowledge effort that demonstrates passion, and show grace when mistakes are made.

Perhaps what we may well have forgotten is found in the Golden Rule. The quote from Confucius is an accurate statement that reflects the message contained in the Golden Rule. Treating someone with respect and trust is certainly the way we want to be treated. Serving, sharing, listening, and caring have everything to do with this strong bond that is genuine and vital. The partnership of the board, the head, and staff all contribute significantly to the school's success. And in the end, nothing is more important than that!

The org. chart does not reflect working together as a team.

ACKNOWLEDGMENTS

After writing *The Board Game* and *Super Boards* I did not intend to write another book addressing the topic of governing boards and their impact on schools and nonprofit organizations. However, as I began my tenure as head of school for the third time in my career, I was thrust once more into the challenges and issues that occupy the world of independent and faith-based schools. As opportunities for professional development occurred, it was increasingly clear that heads of schools were having a difficult time with their boards and trustees needed assistance understanding their roles and responsibilities.

I was often asked to facilitate retreats, lead workshops, and present webinars. It was clear the issues were not going away. In fact, they were becoming more numerous and complicated. Governance concerns in independent schools and faith-based schools continue to be an enormous challenge, and in surveys they always rank near the top of the list of biggest worries.

Increasingly what we describe as best practices is taking a back seat and is being replaced with the idea that the agenda, attitude, behavior, and self-serving egos are surfacing at an alarming rate. I continue to hear from colleagues across the country of situations where board authority and power is being abused at a great cost to the head of school and a greater cost to the school, but it is the students who end up losing the most.

With *Healthy Boards, Successful Schools* I believed it was important to focus exclusively on independent, private, and faith-based schools of all types, sizes, and organizational structures. Every example, description, case story, and situation needed to be completely identifiable with these schools. My hope is that every reader who draws on his or her experiences as a head, trustee, or any other kind of school leader will recognize and connect with this material.

During the research and ultimately writing of this book, I once again reached out to many colleagues, both heads and trustees, in an attempt to be fair, to be accurate, and to communicate in the most meaningful way possible. I have been fortunate to have had the input of many individuals whose distinguished careers in the universe of independent and faith-based schools I benefitted from. I am profoundly grateful for their numerous observations and suggestions. They have collectively made for a far better book than I would have otherwise produced.

Once again, I owe gratitude and sincere thanks for the help, support, interest, encouragement, and creative direction so skillfully provided by my publisher Dan Wright of Fitting Words. Dan has been with me on all three book journeys and his professional attention to detail and personal friendship mean much. My thanks as well to the world's best editor Kyle Olund. Like Dan, Kyle has been on this team from the beginning. The combined knowledge and wisdom of these two book brainiacs has taken me further than I ever thought possible. Their efforts have made all the difference, and I am enormously grateful for their support. In addition to Kyle and Dan, I wish to express my appreciation to my colleague and friend, Dr. Kelley Pujol. Kelley agreed to review the manuscript and her work certainly made Kyle's job much easier. I'm thankful for her wise counsel, excellent judgment, and ability to connect with what I tried to accomplish.

I would like to express my profound thanks and appreciation to Dr. Jeff Jackson, President of the Georgia Independent School Association (GISA). His compelling Foreword to this book will certainly resonant with independent and faith-based school leaders everywhere. It is a special honor to count Jeff as a trusted friend and colleague. His leadership is widely recognized and deeply respected. He has honored me on several occasions to be a presenter and workshop leader for GISA. It is always a privilege to do. Jeff's contributions to the world of independent and faith-based schools continues to be significant and his contribution to this book is substantial.

In the course of one's career there are those who stand apart for their leadership and the impact they have on independent schools. It has been a pleasure to know and learn from Dr. Kirk Walker. His experience and expertise regarding independent school governance has been an inspiration to me and many other heads and trustees. I have borrowed heavily from his wisdom and am grateful for how he has informed my thinking on this topic.

To those of you who wrote an endorsement, thank you for your words of encouragement and support. Your work and careers inspire me, and I am enormously grateful for your contribution to Healthy Boards, Successful Schools.

To everyone whom I have met and talked with over the past two years, I thank you for your candor, insight, and willingness to share your wisdom regarding governance, board development, and looking at what it takes to create and maintain a viable and vibrant board of trustees. You give me great hope for a brighter tomorrow. While I can't identify everyone, here a few whom I would like to especially thank for their support, encouragement, advice, and counsel: David Bass, David Colon, Stan Whitlock, Hugh Harris, Tim Johnson, Scott Parrish, Rick Newberry, Andy Sheets, Pete Majors, Larry McLemore, and Ken Cheeseman.

I would also like to express my deepest appreciation to my colleagues at Providence Christian Academy and to an incredible group of trustees under the leadership of board chair, Julie Knox. If every board were like this board, there would be no need to write this book.

This book is dedicated to my wife Courtney. She is the inspiration for everything I do. Supportive, encouraging, and loving in ways far beyond what I deserve. The book is also dedicated to my mother, Edith Whitehead Mott. She recently passed away and throughout her life, she was one of my biggest fans and strongest advocates. Mother never gave up on me although I gave her many reasons to do so as I grew up. I am blessed beyond what anyone could ever hope for.

Throughout my life and career, I have tried to make a positive difference and to give back, as I have been blessed by so many. This book is my attempt to recognize the vital work done at independent and faith-based schools not only in this country but around the world. Governance and leadership is central to the success of these schools. We must be about the business of getting it right. The stakes are too high to do otherwise. Perhaps this book will be a contribution to that discussion.

About the Author

William R. Mott, Ph.D.

Head of School
Governance Solutions

Williiam R. Mott, Ph.D., works with many independent and faith-based schools and school organizations and associations by conducting workshops, seminars, webinars, etc. on a range of topics and issues that address governance, fundraising, marketing, and leadership challenges.

Dr. Mott's focus is on governance, specifically the connection between independent school boards and the school's senior leadership. Working with boards to deepen their relationship with the school is central to his efforts. His three books, *Healthy Boards, Successful Schools; Super Boards; and The Board Game,* in conjunction with his blog and workshops, reflect this passion and concentration.

His leadership roles include serving as head of three different independent schools, a university director of development, and many years as founder of his own consulting firm. In addition, Dr. Mott has served as trustee at several independent and faith-based schools as well as other nonprofit organizations.

Dr. Mott received his master's and Ph.D. in educational leadership from Vanderbilt University's Peabody College. His B.A. is from the University of Mississippi. He is a graduate of an independent school, Battle Ground Academy in Franklin, Tennessee.

Help for Your Governance Challenges

The Strategic Role of Governance

Board Retreats • Consulting • Presentations

As Dr. Mott has identified in his other books, *Super Boards* and *The Board Game*, the relationship between the head of school and the governing board is the single largest contributor to the success of the independent or faith-based school. Their leadership will be the determining factor in the realization of the mission and vision.

As a result, Dr. Mott's work extends beyond the writing of these three books. It also includes working with schools and nonprofit organizations to achieve success. Specifically, Dr. Mott provides the services and support to be the change needed.

Using *Healthy Boards, Successful Schools, Super Boards* and *The Board Game* as the backdrop for meaningful conversations with school leaders, Dr. Mott will conduct a retreat to include the head of school (as well as key senior staff) and the governing board. While the retreat may have multiple objectives, the overriding objective is to address a range of issues that serve to strengthen the relationship between these groups.

This retreat will produce the following outcomes:

- Identify and resolves key issues that can significantly enhance your school.
- Create a roadmap that provides ways in which the leadership of the staff and board can work effectively and productively.
- Review and revises bylaws and other documents to ensure school mission and vision are reflected in the documents utilized.
- Utilize interactive exercises and case stories to establish areas of concern and areas of strength.
- Provide action steps to ensure that the leadership recognizes warning signs and how to address each one.
- Establish the seven characteristics that bring about meaningful partnerships.
- Encourage adoption and use of the six principles contained in the Governance Promise.
- Encourage the utilization of the Covenant Agreement to establish a working relationship between and among the board and staff.

In addition to the board retreat, Dr. Mott works with the schools in training new board members through a board orientation session or seminar. Dr. Mott also provides coaching in his work with school heads, along with governing board chairs, and others on the board.

Dr. Mott is available for presentations, workshops, and seminars for independent and faith-based schools and school organizations and associations. Speaking engagements may be customized to fit both the topic and time available.

If you want to learn more, contact Dr. Mott at:

Bill@WilliamRMottPhD.com

www.WilliamRMottPhD.com

2000 Mallory Lane

Ste. 130-214

Franklin, TN 37067

ENHANCE YOUR EXPERIENCE

Case Studies, Q&A, and Much More!

A re you interested in enhancing your experience with *Healthy Boards, Successful Schools*? Wouldn't it be great if Dr. Mott could work with you and your school and go more in-depth with the case stories found throughout the book *and* discuss the questions found at the end of each of the stories? In addition, Dr. Mott will assist you and your school regarding other questions and issues you have with governance and board development.

Here is how it works: Call, e-mail, or text Dr. Mott to set up a time once a week or once a month to talk. After you have established a time frame, just set up a conference call for one hour, and Dr. Mott will visit by phone and assist your school with issues through discussion with the head, board chair, committee chair, or any board member. The frequency of your conversations with Dr. Mott will determine your fee.

This is an easy and straightforward way to benefit from Dr. Mott's more than thirty years of experience as a head of school, board member, consultant, author, and speaker. Contact Dr. Mott today and begin creating the healthiest board possible for your school!